2021 EDITION

# COLLEGE READY

### EXPERT ADVICE FOR PARENTS TO SIMPLIFY THE COLLEGE TRANSITION

EDITED BY
**CHELSEA PETREE, Ph.D.**

# WISE**ACTION**

Published by Wise Action
201 N. Union Street, Suite 110
Alexandria, Virginia 22301
https://wiseaction.co

Wise Action and design are trademarks of Wise Action Company.

The publisher is not responsible for websites (or their contents) that are not owned by the publisher.

ISBN: 978-1-7369182-0-3 (paperback)
ISBN: 978-1-7369182-3-4 (paperback)
ISBN: 978-1-7369182-1-0 (ebook);
ISBN: 978-1-7369182-2-7 (ePub)

Bulk Purchases. Quantity discounts are available. Please make inquiries via https://collegeready.guide

# Table of Contents

*This book is dedicated to the parents, siblings, family members, caregivers, mentors, and all supporters of college-bound students as you embark on this exciting new journey.*

# Contributors

## Editor

**Chelsea Petree, Ph.D.**
**Rochester Institute of Technology**

Chelsea Petree is the Parent & Family Programs Director at Rochester Institute of Technology (RIT). Chelsea moved to Rochester in 2015 to establish the Parent & Family Programs office, including developing a comprehensive parent communications plan and implementing family events and engagement opportunities. She has worked to establish a "parents as partners" culture at RIT, increasing support of families across the institution. Chelsea received her Ph.D. in Family Social Science from the University of Minnesota in 2013 and serves as the president of AHEPPP: Family Engagement in Higher Education, where she is proud to lead the organization and create new opportunities to support and build community with its members. Prior to being elected into this role, she was actively involved in AHEPPP for many years as a volunteer, member of the Conference Planning Committee, webinar and conference presenter, mentor, and the AHEPPP Journal and Insights blog editor.

# Authors

**Kristin Austin, Ed.D.**
**West Chester University of PA**

Kristin Austin has been working in higher education in enrollment and transition capacities for more than 18 years. Kristin's dissertation focused on parental support during first-year college transition, and she eagerly views parents as partners in student success. With experiences in public, private, international, small, and large institutions, Kristin has observed that all parents have the same goal: to launch healthy, successful, well-adjusted adults.

**Lady Cox, Ed.D.**
**Auburn University**

Lady Cox is the Associate Vice President for Student Affairs at Auburn University, where she leads the following units: First Year Experience, Greek Life, Health Promotion and Wellness Services, Student Conduct, Student Counseling and Psychological Services, and Student Involvement. Lady is a longtime advocate for parents. She created the Parent and Family Program offices at both Mississippi State University and Auburn. Lady has a bachelor's degree from Mississippi State, a master's degree from Auburn, and a doctorate from the University of Georgia.

**Libby Daggers**
**Texas A&M University**

Libby Daggers serves as the Coordinator for Parent & Family Programming at Texas A&M University and has worked with Aggie families since July 2012. Libby holds a bachelor's degree from the University of Illinois, a master's degree from Illinois State University, and is pursuing a Ph.D. in Higher Education Administration at

Texas A&M. Libby serves as a Regional Chair for AHEPPP: Family Engagement in Higher Education.

## Maureen Hurley
## Emerson College

Maureen Hurley is part of the campus life team at Emerson College in Boston, where she oversees Student Transitions and Family Programs. Maureen has been at Emerson for almost four years and loves the creative vibe that runs through the community. Prior to her arrival at Emerson, she worked at her alma mater, Boston University, where she earned both an undergraduate and graduate degree. She also worked for the British School of Boston as the Director of Admissions. Maureen serves on the Board of Directors of AHEPPP: Family Engagement in Higher Education.

## Nicki Jenkins
## University of Kentucky

Nicki Jenkins is the Senior Program Specialist for the Parent and Family Association at the University of Kentucky. Nicki has been at UK for almost six years, welcoming, educating, and connecting parents and family members. Prior to her arrival at UK, Nicki served in various roles supporting student and family activities at the College of Charleston, the University of Maine, and NC State University. She recognizes the critical role parents and families play in supporting students and enjoys being able to contribute to their successful transition to college. Nicki has a master's degree from the University of Maine and plans to pursue a Ph.D. in higher education. She has previously been a member of the AHEPPP: Family Engagement in Higher Education Conference Planning Committee (2017–2019), and served as the committee chair in 2019.

**Andrea Mitchen**
**University of Houston**

Andrea Mitchen has been in higher education administration for approximately 18 years. After graduating from Winthrop University in Rock Hill, South Carolina, she worked for her international sorority for a year as a leadership consultant before pursuing her master's degree in Student Affairs Administration in Higher Education at Ball State University. Upon graduating, Andrea moved to Texas and has worked at two large, public universities and a two-year college in the Houston area. She has been at the University of Houston for five years and enjoys supporting parents and families of students because she was a first-generation student. She understands the importance of not only having support for students but the supporters having the information they need to provide the support. Andrea serves on the Board of Directors of AHEPPP: Family Engagement in Higher Education.

**Mark Pontious, Ph.D.**
**Miami University**

Mark Pontious serves as Miami University's Director of Parent & Family Programs, a position which he has held since October 2014. Mark has worked in higher education since 2007, primarily in the field of family engagement. Mark holds a bachelor's degree from Bowling Green State University, a master's degree from Florida State University, and a Ph.D. in Educational Leadership from Miami. Mark is a member of the AHEPPP: Family Engagement in Higher Education Conference Planning Committee.

## Christine Self, Ph.D.
## Texas Tech University

Christine Self has worked in parent and family programming since 2002 and currently serves as the Associate Director for Parent & Family Relations at Texas Tech University. Christine holds three degrees from Texas Tech University: a bachelor's degree in General Studies, a master's degree in Higher Education Administration, and a Ph.D. in Higher Education Research with a certificate in Women's and Gender Studies. Christine serves as the AHEPPP: Family Engagement in Higher Education representative on the Council for the Advancement of Standards in Higher Education (CAS).

## Stephanie Stiltner
## University of Pikeville

Stephanie Stiltner is the Director of Family Connections at the University of Pikeville (UPIKE) in Kentucky, a program she had the opportunity to develop in 2018. Her previous experience in higher education includes serving in the university's Office of Public Affairs, where she developed a diverse skill set and widespread knowledge about the institution, both of which she puts to use every day as she serves families. She holds bachelor's and master's degrees in Communication. Stephanie is a member of the AHEPPP: Family Engagement in Higher Education Conference Planning Committee.

## Amy Swank
## Bowling Green State University

Amy Swank is the Director of Parent, Family and New Student Connections at Bowling Green State University and has been involved in higher education for 14 years. She recognizes the level of involvement parents/family members seek and expect in the university lives of their students. By providing appropriate avenues to stay connected to the university, and addressing questions and concerns related to their student's needs, she has been able to forge positive and lasting relationships with the parents and families she serves. Amy is the Past President of AHEPPP: Family Engagement in Higher Education.

### Brie Jutte Waterman
### University of Colorado Boulder

Brie Jutte Waterman is a Program Coordinator in New Student & Family Programs at the University of Colorado Boulder. Brie graduated from Kansas State University in 2017 with her master of science in College Student Development and from Kent State University in 2015 with her bachelor of arts in Communication Studies. Brie is a member of the AHEPPP: Family Engagement in Higher Education Conference Planning Committee.

### Benjamin M. Williams
### Georgia State

Benjamin M. Williams oversees Orientation, Parent & Family Programs, and Off-Campus Housing across Georgia State's six campuses. He is a proud alumnus of Georgia State and spends his days supporting members of the New Student Orientation Team in their efforts to welcome and support the successful transitions of students and families. Ben is working on his Ph.D. in Education Policy Studies, focused on equity and student success in higher education. He serves as a Regional Chair for AHEPPP: Family Engagement in Higher Education.

**Kesha Williams**
**Johns Hopkins University**

Kesha Williams is the Director for Parent and Family Relations for Johns Hopkins University. In this role, Kesha focuses on overseeing parent and family communications, promoting information about campus resources, creating an interactive role for parents and families within the campus community and beyond, and serving as a resource for parents and families as well as other university units. Kesha has been working with families in higher education for over 12 years. She obtained a bachelor of science and a master's degree in Health Education and Recreation from Southern Illinois University Carbondale. Kesha served on the Board of Directors of AHEPPP: Family Engagement in Higher Education from 2013–2017.

# Preface

My niece Joey is in preschool. At least once a week, my sister shares a photo she received about Joey's day—what she's eating for lunch, the projects she's working on, and what she's playing on the playground. Parents like my sister now receive constant updates about their child's day through apps, texts, or portals, starting from the first day of preschool or day care. The advent of the parent portal has provided parents and caregivers the ability to monitor a child's every bite, friend, and macaroni art project. I love these glimpses into Joey's life, and know that parents love to feel connected to their children when they are not in sight.

Every time I get a picture, however, I can't help but think ahead, to the day preschoolers like Joey will step onto the college campus of their choice and suddenly, before parents know what happened, be "adults." After 12+ years of access, parents will no longer be able to see what their children are eating, how they did on an assignment, and who they're hanging out with.

This is where I come in. I have a job that most people don't know exists. My job title has the word "parent" in it, which can be surprising for those who read the horror stories in the media about helicopter parents and believe that the college experience should only include the student. My job—and others who work in parent and family programs across the country—is to bridge the gap between you, your student, and the university. I am here to support you as you support your student. I provide opportunities for you to engage in the campus community, while making sure you understand that this is a time when your student needs to gain independence. I find it an honor to work with Rochester Institute of Technology families every day (whom I lovingly refer to as "my parents").

You may have just read a few words related to your student that make you nervous, like "access," "adult," and "independence." While it's true that the transition to college will be a big one for your entire family, rest assured that it doesn't happen overnight. You have time to make the adjustment, starting with this summer. Think of this summer as a dry run: your student can practice making their own doctor's appointments and filling out forms, and you can practice coaching them on how to find answers to their questions on their own. Practicing this now will prepare you for that big day in the near future when you move them into their dorm room or send your commuter off to class.

This year, more than ever, it might feel extra nerve-wracking to think of launching your (nearly adult) baby into the world. In 2020, scary "what ifs" that we never expected to happen happened. The entire world came to halt, then pivoted, and we managed to make it through the year— in sometimes less than ideal ways—to make it to today. Your student experienced losses and setbacks. You may be worried that they aren't prepared for college and all of the responsibilities that come with it.

Sending them to college this year will take a lot of trust. You need to trust that your student has developed the resiliency to get through more tough times in the future. You need to trust that the college will be their safety net when they need extra support. You need to trust in yourself, and all of the lessons you have provided over the past 18 years. It's time to let them grow and take control of their own future. But parents—they still need you. They need your advice, your encouragement, your reminders, and your love.

The goal of this book is to help you through this summer and all of the preparations you have ahead of you. While your family is wrapping up high school events and graduation parties, you will also be helping your student fill out college forms and shop for their dorm room. There will be honest and difficult conversations to have, and everyone's emotions will be high at times. It's a lot to balance, and it might be overwhelming to know where to start and how to prioritize. We are here to help.

I am so grateful for the authors of this book, who are truly THE experts in the field of family engagement. They have been working with families like yours for years, and their advice is priceless. I am lucky to call them my colleagues, partners, and friends.

I am thankful for the thorough review of my copyeditor, Sabrina Detlef, and our publisher, Wise Action, who brought an idea to me and worked hard to make it a reality. AHEPPP: Family Engagement in Higher Education not only provided the authors for this book, but brings the entire field together in the promotion of parents as campus partners. This book would not have been possible without the support and wisdom of Lindsay McKinney, the best Executive Director I could imagine having by my side.

Finally, parents and family members, thank YOU for all of the hard work you have put into supporting your student and getting them to this point. We can't wait to see them on campus this fall!

**Chelsea Petree, Ph.D.**
*College Ready* **Editor**
**Director, Parent & Family Programs**
**Rochester Institute of Technology**

# Introduction

If you are the parent, family member, caregiver, sibling, mentor, or support of a soon-to-be college student, this book is for you.

This summer will truly be a unique experience for your family. Sending a student to college can change your family dynamics, your household structure, and the way you spend your time and money. This college experience will be different from anything you experienced yourself, or anything you have experienced with other children, as each college student's journey is individual. This year brings an added level of newness to the college experience, as it comes on the heels of the global pandemic that has shaped the way your family has lived and learned since early 2020. Your student's high school experience ended in ways you didn't expect, and their college experience will begin with some unknowns. You have additional reasons to want to be extra prepared this summer, and *College Ready* will help you navigate this process.

Each author of *College Ready* is a college administrator who has worked extensively with parents and families of students. They are all members of AHEPPP: Family Engagement in Higher Education, the only professional association in the world dedicated to parent/family involvement in the college experience. These authors are experts in the field overall and in the particular chapters they penned.

The chapters that follow cover many of the topics that you are thinking about as you continue your college preparations. Beginning with the initial steps after college acceptance and moving through that first visit home in the fall, this book will serve as your guide. It will describe what to expect in a variety of areas and things to look for as you navigate all of the information that will come from your student's college this summer. The longer your student is in college, the more your family will settle in, get into routines, and understand your university's processes. These first several months, however, will be filled with questions, transitions, and lessons.

While there are emotional parts to this process, this particular book focuses on action items, rather than tips on how to "let go" of your child. Some information might seem obvious, while other pieces will be eye-opening. Every family is different, and pieces of the book will resonate differently with each reader. The new information can help you plan, and the things you already knew should assure you that you are on the right track.

Each chapter concludes with a list of conversation starters. These prompts will help you think of how to talk to your student about specific topics. In thinking how to use them, consider your relationship, family dynamics, and student's history. Using open-ended questions is the best way to get information from your student. Not only will having these conversations assist you in your college preparations, but they will also open new lines of communication that can continue when the semester begins.

The appendices include checklists that will keep you on track throughout this summer and into the semester. These lists contain some items that are standard for all incoming students—regardless of where they will be attending—but also what you as a parent can do to support this transition. Through all of your preparations, conversations, and planning, remember to have patience with your family. This year was hard, and parts of the future are unknown, but you made it here. It is time for your college journey to begin.

# Chapter 1

# WE'VE PICKED A SCHOOL; NOW WHAT?

## How to get through the next few steps

**Kesha Williams**
**Johns Hopkins University**

Congratulations! Your child has made their college choice and was accepted. What an accomplishment! This is an exciting time for you and your family. But what are the next steps? There is so much to think about. The idea of your student leaving home for an extended period can seem scary. There are plenty of questions going through your mind as a parent: Did I prepare them properly? Will they be okay? What do we do next?

Your student will grow a lot in the coming months, and you get a front row seat in watching the transition into adulthood. The summer will move pretty quickly. Here are some next steps to get you and your family members organized.

## Keep a Calendar

Your family calendar can consist of important college deadlines for the summer as well as scheduled family time. Be mindful that the excitement of high school isn't quite over yet, and you and your student should enjoy all the events that are planned. A great location to put a paper calendar is the kitchen, a room everyone frequents. We know how much teenagers like to eat! You can also keep an electronic calendar online that everyone shares. Be sure to set a recurring meeting to plan for the college transition at regular intervals, like weekly.

Visit the university's website and find the academic calendar, which is normally located on the registrars and records web page, so you can mark down dates like move-in, the first day of classes, and orientation. You can call it the "Countdown to College." Make sure to include dates for family check-ins to discuss what each of you accomplished that week in your college prep.

## Plan a Second Visit

One of the immediate things you should try and do is visit the campus again, in person if possible or through virtual options offered by admissions and other offices. Your student's post-acceptance visit will allow for an even more relevant picture of life on their chosen campus. Also, if your student hasn't already made living arrangements, a second visit will allow them to select accommodations. It might not be feasible to visit the inside of a residence hall, but you will get a feel for how the building looks from the outside and how the communal space functions. Many housing offices have virtual tours or photos of building options on their websites.

You and your student should take that opportunity to set up some appointments to speak with administrators or faculty from the department of your student's area of study. This is also the time to mix and mingle with as many current students as you can to learn about clubs and organizations that target academic, social, or athletic interests. Participating in an organization is a great way for your student to network, but also build great leadership skills. Families who support students who identify with or want to explore an underrepresented group should visit offices that specifically engage, develop, and help these students excel and celebrate who they are in the community. This is an important factor for student development. College is a time where students find out who they are and get a chance to interact with people who are different but also like-minded.

Lastly, it's a chance to get excited! You can learn the location, go to a game, find all the great dining facilities on and near campus, and still stop by admissions to find out if any new cool programs or events like family weekend are planned. Be sure to stop at the bookstore and buy your student a shirt to show off where they are headed in the fall!

## Communicate Openly

Communication is paramount in every relationship. It is especially important while making the transition to a university. During your scheduled family time, confirm with your student that they have received a personalized email address from the university and stress the importance of checking their school email account frequently. This is the school's main method of communication and it's essential to not missing important deadlines.

Dynamics will and should start to change within your family. In college, student information is protected by law (see chapter 3), but your student does have the ability to grant access to family members. Be sure to communicate about what types of access you will be granted. This conversation allows you and your student to manage expectations as to what they are responsible for and what you expect access to (e.g., access to the bill or to final grades). Family members and students should articulate and be transparent about their expectations of each other as it relates to the first year of college.

Give yourself grace and acknowledge that you will have some fears and apprehension. That is okay. It's normal and you are human—and so is your student. As you allow your student to make decisions, they will start to learn and practice critical thinking skills. These are essential to becoming a young adult. They won't always get it right on the first try.

You should feel confident that you provided a great blueprint for success. During those times when you thought they weren't listening, they were, and you will be surprised how much they reminisce, use, or seek your advice when experiencing challenges or making critical decisions. The important thing is to step back and let your student take the lead. You should start to take the role of advisor as they start to learn how to manage their own life.

## Important Campus Partners

For some families, it may not be feasible for you to re-visit the campus. This is perfectly okay. Universities have websites that offer a plethora of information to help incoming students and families. Encourage your student to research and familiarize themselves with the following departments. You can discuss this during the scheduled family meetings. Note that office names will vary by college.

- **Orientation/First-Year Experience.** Orientation plays an integral role in the transition into the university. Orientation programs normally reach out to students in the spring. This helps families understand how to prepare and what will be required of the student. This is often the student's first opportunity to meet classmates in a more personal setting and make connections. For families, orientation is not required, but it is highly recommended. These programs are designed to help you to learn more about the university and engage with many of the departments and administrators that will make an impact during the college journey. Students and families will learn about a variety of resources to help them succeed.

- **Parent and Family Programs.** Families, like students, are going through a transition. If your campus has one, the parent and family programs office provides communications, services, and programs (e.g., family weekend) while your student is in college. It provides family members with information so that they can better support their students. Family members should ensure they get the newsletter and other relevant information, and participate as much as they can and in whatever ways they can. Look for opportunities to get involved like volunteering for family programs or giving back philanthropically.

- **Registrars and Records.** This office acts as the keeper of all student records at the university: student transcripts, grades, classes, and biographical information.

- **Financial Aid.** This office provides students with financial resources. Those resources can include scholarships, grants, loans, or student work jobs. Financial aid advisors are assigned to students to assist them based on student or family needs.

- **Student Accounts.** This office manages your student's bill/account (often called the bursar's office or financial services). Families or students can pay their entire bill when it's due, or make arrangements with the university to schedule payments. This website is where you will also find tuition, housing, and student fee costs. It will also have the important dates of when bills are due.

- **Housing/Residential Life.** The university housing office manages the on-campus residence halls and apartments that students live in while in college. They are responsible for the maintenance of the building. Students also have residential hall directors and student resident assistants (RAs) who develop programs for students and help them interact with their peers.

- **Dining.** This is where you will find all the dining options for your student. There are usually many that are offered that will fit a variety of preferences. When picking a dining plan, talk realistically about what meals your student normally likes to eat. This will help determine what meal plan they should choose.

- **Culture and Community Centers.** There are many offices on campus that build community and offer support to different populations. These can include: multicultural centers, spirituality and religious life, women's centers, LGBTQA+ offices, diversity and inclusion offices, etc. Your student will learn about these at orientation and during welcome week activities, but should also reach out this summer to learn about programming and get connected.

- **Student Health/Counseling Center.** At any university, students' health is the university's number one priority. While it's important they keep up with their classes, it's also important that they keep a healthy mind, body, and soul. Speak with your student about identifying and understanding what programs, applications, and facilities are available to promote a balanced, healthy lifestyle. Also, talk to your student about finding out about what resources (such as support groups and counseling services) are available and how they work with your student's insurance.

- **Academic Support and Outreach.** These offices are designated to assist students with any academic support they may need with their classes. This would include tutoring, study groups, or help with the various study subjects on campus, such as a campus writing center. It's important to identify these resources, discuss when to use them, and understand how to access them early to ensure success.

- **Advising Office.** The advising office plays an integral role in a student's college experience. It advises students on what classes they should take, monitors their progress, and helps them fulfill class requirements so that they can graduate. The best student-advisor relationship centers around partnership. Once an advisor has been assigned to your student, encourage them to do regular check-ins, such as on a quarterly or semesterly basis. Students need to understand the requirements of the course of study in which they are majoring and use advising time to get their questions answered.

## Closing Advice

There is a lot to accomplish over the summer, but with a little organization and open communication, your family will be fine! Your student is ready for this new step and so are you. Make sure you both are checking (and reading) emails and completing all necessary steps. Don't be afraid to reach out to the university with questions. Finally, find time to have fun and enjoy one another's company.

## Conversation Starters

- What day of the week works best for conversions about college prep?

- What social events do you have planned that we can add to the family calendar?

- How can I support you in completing your college checklist?

- Is your college open for visits this summer?

- What is your school email address?

- What have you heard about orientation?

# Chapter 2
# HOW DO WE MAKE THE MOST OF THIS SUMMER?

How to balance family and student expectations

## Amy Swank
## Bowling Green State University

You may notice your student acts a little differently this summer. After graduating from high school, students feel grown up and ready to move on from their childhood environment. They may seem to have little time and patience for family and feel too mature for old routines and house rules. You might also find that your student is not around much. They are not just saying goodbye to family, but also to friends and high school classmates, all while wrapping up high school activities, working a summer job, and preparing for college.

You may feel a mix of emotions. One day you wish this summer will never end, and the next you want it to hurry up so you can ship your student off to college. You will find yourself reflecting on the individual moments that got you here and if you—and your student—are ready for this next step.

These next few months are an important time to continue critical conversations, provide some guidance, and set expectations for the new normal you will experience as a college family. It may be challenging, though, to balance all of the wants and needs over the summer, such as your desire for family time to enjoy those "lasts," your student's desire for time with their friends, the need to shop for dorm room supplies, and your student's wish for more freedom to practice adult responsibilities. Here are some tips for creating balance and making the most of your last summer together before college.

## Celebrate the End of High School

Your student will have clear college deadlines, such as registering for orientation and choosing a room. While it's important to pay attention to these deadlines, don't forget to celebrate the end of high school and all of the accomplishments that come with it. The award banquets, last games, final concerts, and, of course, high school graduation should be celebrated on their own, not in the shadow of what is to come.

Be aware of what can be called "last-time syndrome." There will be moments this summer when you realize it's a last for your family before your student moves to college. Make the most of these moments, even though they may also cause some sadness and/or frustration. If you get an eye roll when expressing your emotions, remember your student is also experiencing many "lasts" and may be expressing these emotions differently.

## Focus on Family Time

This might not be the last summer your student is home with you. In fact, it's likely they will return over the summer for at least the first year. However, it will feel different then, as they get busier, are more engaged in their own activities, and become more independent. Take advantage of these months together to do all the things your family loves to do as a family and maybe haven't had time for this last year. Whether this is a vacation, a family game night, weekly dinners where no phones are allowed at the table, or visiting a local amusement park, you will be glad you made time for family bonding time when the semester is in full swing and you are missing your student.

## Plan Goodbyes Now

It may feel way too early to think about saying goodbye, but the last thing you want is for your student to leave a farewell dinner with their grandparents early because their best friend from high school is having a send-off party that same evening. As suggested in chapter 1, it's important to keep a shared family calendar and include events like parties, with both family and friends. Set expectations about the last few evenings before move-in day. If you expect your student to be at home for family time, tell them now so they can make alternative plans with friends. Remember to compromise and make sure your student has time with both family and friends.

## Encourage Sibling Time

Younger siblings often feel neglected as their older brother or sister heads to college. These last few months are all about your soon-to-be college student—the final high school events, graduation ceremonies, focused time completing the college checklist, and shopping for their dorm room. You know you will need to pay extra attention to younger siblings following move-in day, but you should also include them in the excitement throughout the summer. Ask them questions about their next year in school, and, if they are in high school, what they are thinking about in terms of colleges. Maybe now is a good time to let them redecorate their bedroom. Invite them on move-in day if possible. Encourage your college-bound student to make special time for younger siblings, reminding them of how much they will miss that relationship once it is primarily on Snapchat and TikTok, and not around the dinner table.

## Start Having Difficult Conversations

As you read this book, you will develop a list of things to discuss with your student over the summer. Don't wait until the last minute, especially for the tough conversations that may take several attempts. When you engage with your student on difficult topics, they are more likely to consider your opinion when making decisions. Silence, however, also sends a strong message. College should be a time when students are excited about their new freedoms but they will also be a little nervous about how to establish themselves in a whole new environment.

As you prepare for your student to leave home, set aside some time to talk with them in person. Keep your reactions and tone in check and discuss your expectations. Find teachable moments from television, books, or current events. Any of these topics can positively or negatively affect a student's success in college. Remember that difficult conversations are ongoing and you should continue to talk with your student after they arrive on campus and beyond. If you see dramatic changes in your student once they are on campus, be prepared to find support at their college or university.

## Begin to Shift Household Responsibilities

Your student likely has responsibilities around the house, whether that be keeping their room clean, walking the dog, or mowing the lawn. This summer, begin to think of how to transition some of these responsibilities to other family members in preparation for your college student to move away. Even if your student will be living at home and commuting or learning virtually, remember that their schedule will be very different than in high school and some adjustments are likely needed.

As you shift these chores, remind your student of the things they will be responsible for in college and focus on those. For example, they will have to take the trash out of their residence hall room or apartment to avoid bugs and odors; make sure they are already used to this chore. You won't be there to change and wash their sheets; help them understand how often they should be doing this and encourage them to practice this now (though don't be surprised if the sheets haven't been changed when you pick them up for Thanksgiving break!). If they'll have a car on campus, be sure they are in charge of filling the tank over the summer and checking the tire pressure.

## Give More Freedom

In a few short months, your student will begin managing their everyday routines and time, learning in a new environment and experimenting with new ideas, friends, and opportunities. While it will be scary to let go in this way, help them understand how to be responsible in college by granting some additional freedoms now. This could mean an extended curfew, letting them keep their own schedule (even when you're aching to wake them up before noon), and only checking in about college-related tasks once a week, rather than every day.

Granting new freedoms does not have to mean eliminating check-ins. Let your student know when you expect a check-in (e.g., "if you're going to be out past midnight, I expect a text"). Establishing expectations such as these now will help set a standard of communications and check-ins once they are on their own.

Let them grow. Allow them to begin their adventure of self-discovery and development and decide how you are going to handle this new stage of life.

## Start Guiding from the Sideline

One thing you will see throughout this book, regardless of the chapter topic, is the need to begin to let your student take the lead. You will also hear this in your family orientation programming in phrases like "Be the coach, not the player" or "You're now a passenger, not the driver." It's time that you become a guide from the side who promotes independence through problem-solving. Your student needs your support, but also needs to do the work themselves. This will continue throughout their time in college, as students often call parents with the challenges they face and to vent.

This summer is the perfect time to encourage your student to take the lead. When they come to you with a question or a task they aren't sure how to handle, help them resolve the problem with questions such as:

- What are the resources that can help answer that question?
- Did you try to research that on the school website?
- What are some questions you can ask to learn more?
- How did you handle [a similar challenge] in high school?

It won't be easy to make the transition to the guide and listener, but you are developing long-term skills that will help your student build problem-solving skills and develop independence. Practicing this summer will make it easier when they aren't right there. Remember too, that the first question you ask yourself should always be, "Is this an emergency?" (Note that your student's idea of an emergency may be different from yours and the institution's.)

## Closing Advice

This summer will go fast. There is a lot to do and a lot to balance. Remember, even during the difficult moments, that you will miss your student. Make the most of your time together. Be patient and understanding. Be excited about everything your student is about to experience and the ways in which they will grow. Remember to use your sense of humor! Make sure they hear your excitement and let them know they will be missed. Finally, remember that it isn't just your student experiencing a transition, but you and other family members as well.

---

### Conversation Starters

- How will you let me know if you're going to miss curfew?

- What household chores will you be responsible for in your college living space?

- When are your final concerts/games/etc.?

- When are your friends leaving for school and how will you say goodbye?

- What are your favorite things that we do together as a family?

---

## Chapter 3
# WILL I BE ABLE TO SEE MY STUDENT'S INFORMATION?

How to balance student privacy
and your need for access

**Maureen Hurley**
**Emerson College**

One discovery you may have already made, especially if this is not
your first student in college, is the shift that happens in the handling
of educational records. For your student's first 18 years, you've likely
handled most (if not all) of their educational, medical, and financial
records. What a shock it can be to suddenly not have access anymore!
You may know that the federal regulation that governs these records
is called FERPA (Family Educational Rights and Privacy Act). The
rights that you've perhaps taken for granted transfer to your student,
even if they will still be under 18 upon starting at their chosen college.

What does this mean in practice? It means that your student will
have to give permission to their school to release certain records to
you or anyone else. In the United States, parents have direct access to
homework completion, projects, and grade information in the kindergarten through 12th grade years. Parents may also have enjoyed

frequent communication with teachers, administrators, and guidance counselors. From here on, your student will be in charge of this access and information. As you will see, there is a fine line between your student's privacy and your access to records.

## The Other F Word

FERPA, also referred to as the Buckley Amendment after Senator James Buckley, the lead proponent of it, is a federal law enacted in the wake of the Vietnam War, Watergate hearings, and the resignation of President Richard Nixon. This was a time filled with distrust of the government and also of significant student activism. Students protested against colleges and universities providing personally identifying information (PII) to employers, agencies, other educational institutions, and yes, parents or guardians.

Although many aspects of FERPA apply to children and their families in kindergarten through 12th grade, we'll focus on how it affects you as the parent of a college student. The law gives your student the right to inspect and review their education records; the right to request changes or corrections if they dispute the information that is contained in the record (and to appeal to the U.S. Department of Education if there is no agreement reached); the right to give access to others; and the right to obtain a copy of their records.

## What FERPA Covers

The law is expansive and has been amended several times, but there are three broad categories that it covers: financial records, academic records, and student life. Financial records are just what you'd expect—the bills for tuition, fees, room and board, and any other institutional charges. These records also include details about any scholarships, grants, loans, or other forms of financial assistance your student may have received. Also included in this category are your tax returns and any other information submitted during the financial assistance process. Academic records include the courses your student has taken, grades earned, class standing, and typically your student's advisor and professors' names. The final category, the student life records, encompasses campus standards violations and disciplinary action.

You may be wondering how your student may transfer access to these records to you.

Colleges and universities have different ways of handling these "proxy access" requests. For some schools, a blanket form is available for the student to allow you access to everything. At other schools, a form is available only "situationally." For example, a student may waive rights so that you may speak to the office of accessibility services to discuss their accommodations for a learning difference, but another waiver may need to be signed to access their disciplinary record. Almost universally a proxy is available for you to be able to see and pay the bill!

As with any great regulation, there are exceptions. First, colleges may publish directory-type information without your student's permission. Directory information covers the basics: name, address, and phone number; but it also covers athletic team information such as height and weight. Second, colleges may, *but are not required to*, share information about your student with you if you claim them as a dependent on your tax return. Third, if your student is posing a danger to themselves or the community, or if they have a serious drug or alcohol violation, the school may share this information with you.

## Privacy and Parental Rights

These regulations are dizzying. And they can be implemented in various ways at different institutions; for instance, you could have two students at two colleges and the records may be handled in quite dissimilar ways. But here is one gem: even though a college official may not be able to share information with you, you can share whatever you would like with them!

When you share information about your student's situation with staff members, they will be able to direct you and your student on how to proceed and who to contact without violating FERPA. They cannot confirm or deny what is happening with your student, but can help you understand what steps to take in the situation you explain (e.g., they cannot confirm that your student did or did not fail a class, but they can tell you what happens when a student does fail a class). They will also be able to share more information if your student is on the call. In fact, most offices will prefer a three-way conversation with student, parents, and staff to ensure that everyone hears the same information and is on the same page.

You may be wondering why access to these records is such a big deal. Just as we know that no two students develop at exactly the same rate, some students may be prepared to manage their own records without any parent or family member to assist, while others will not. This shifting of responsibility happens gradually for some, and instantly for others. Besides the law itself, there are other great reasons to have your student begin taking charge of their own records. College is a time when young people prepare for the so-called "real" world. A big part of that means that colleges want to empower them to make a phone call that they would typically ask you to make, complete their own paperwork, and learn where to turn when things don't go as planned. As tempting as it may be to make a call on behalf of your student, it may be better that you encourage them to do it instead. This can be a hard shift in mindset for all involved. As students begin taking on more responsibility for their own needs, they will be better prepared to handle the complexities of life in the future.

You may want to start discussing FERPA with your student before they arrive on campus. It's important for you each to have an understanding of what is expected. There are some parents who say, "if I'm paying the bill, I get to see your grades." Others say, "you're an adult now and you're going to be fully in charge."

Spend some time with your student on the college's website to learn when and how access is handled. This is often covered during orientation programs for students and their family members. These are tricky waters to navigate, but talking about them with your student and understanding the specifics of their college's implementation policies will help you both navigate the waters!

## Frequently Asked Questions about FERPA

*I pay the bill; doesn't that allow me access to my student's records?*

Actually no. Your student will still need to release information to you—including access to the bill itself—even if you are paying for their education.

*If my tax records are used to calculate my student's financial aid, does that mean that they will be able to see this sensitive information?*

No. Although this information is used and is included in the student's file, it will not be released to them. Tax records are held as confidential and protected documents

*My student is only 17 so I'll be able to gain access to everything until they're 18, correct?*

No. FERPA covers all students in postsecondary education, regardless of age. If you have a student who enters college at any point before their 18th birthday, the FERPA law grants them the right to give or retain access to their records.

*What happens if my student has a health/mental health emergency?*

If your student is seriously hurt or ill the school may reach out to you. This is different from sharing health records with you, and many schools will have guidelines about when they contact you. For example, it may be when a student must go to the hospital for treatment. (See chapter 6 for more information about campus health resources.)

*My student has a learning difference and has always been on an Individualized Education Plan (IEP). Can I speak with the office that oversees accommodations?*

If you wanted to speak specifically about your student's accommodations currently, you would need permission. As noted above, you may give information about your student's history, testing, IEPs, and any other information you think important to your student's success. However, the staff member will be constrained about reciprocating information.

*What if my student gets in trouble with alcohol or drugs? Will the college let me know?*

This is another tricky question. The answer is that higher education institutions can, *but do not have to*, make this information available. If your student is under the age of 21, the school is allowed to contact you about these violations. Colleges might have certain guidelines about when to contact parents in these circumstances. For example, you may be notified if your student violated the alcohol policy in such a way that it resulted in their own, or another person's hospitalization.

*Will I be able to speak with my student's professor?*

Under almost all circumstances, parents will not be able to speak with a professor or faculty member. If your student is in a meeting with a professor and a conference call or other method of communication with you has been agreed upon by all parties, such contact may take place, but it would be very unusual. Professors do not have to agree to speak with anyone besides the student.

*Do FERPA laws only apply to citizens of the United States?*

No. The privacy laws apply to all students, regardless of their country of citizenship.

## Closing Advice

Not having access to your student's educational records may be one of the biggest changes for you as a college parent. Don't be afraid of FERPA, and remember that staff members will be able to talk to you about procedures and policies without violating your student's privacy. Talk to your student about your expectations about sharing information, particularly around grades and bills.

---

### Conversation Starters

- Have you thought about what it means to be in charge of your education records?

- Did you know that you will have to give me access to see and pay the tuition and fees?

- Have you read in any college emails about how you can grant me proxy access?

- Will you show me your final grades or will you give me access to them?

---

## Chapter 4

# HOW CAN I HELP MY STUDENT SUCCEED IN CLASS?

## How to support your student academically

**Mark Pontious**
**Miami University**

Many high school students are used to being academically successful without investing a lot of effort in courses. Regardless of high school performance, college-level academic work is an adjustment, both in terms of content and expectations in managing time and responsibilities. Your encouragement and insightful questions are important to a successful academic transition. Remember, this transition looks different for every student and from any college experience you may have had yourself.

Supporting your student's academic transition starts by learning about the expectations at their institution. Take full advantage of any orientation activities on this topic (and make sure they do too). In addition to basics about academic requirements, learn about tutoring, writing assistance, academic advising, and other resources available, so you can tuck them away for later use. Knowing about the academic aspect of your student's institution will help you better support their success.

## Common Academic Terms

- **Academic advisor.** A staff or faculty member who helps students understand and complete degree requirements and meet academic goals. Much of this work is driven by the student, who reaches out to meet with the advisor about course selection and registration, degree requirements and completion, and major exploration. Students are often assigned an advisor before or during their first semester.

- **Academic department and college.** Colleges and universities are often broken down into smaller units with common academic programs called colleges or schools, which are then broken down further into academic departments, which are comprised of majors or groups of similar majors. Colleges are led by a dean and departments are led by a department chair, both of whom are typically faculty members within that unit. Department chairs report to the dean, who in turn typically reports to the chief academic officer, often called a provost.

- **General education requirements.** Most institutions have a common set of requirements all students must fulfill, in addition to requirements in their specific academic major. These requirements stretch across academic fields and usually include courses in writing, mathematics, humanities, fine arts, science, and sometimes intercultural perspective. These courses prepare students for a lifetime of learning and to successfully work with people outside their specific academic area of study.

- **Major.** A specific area of study, in which students take a range of courses. Majors are sometimes, but not always, directly related to a post-college career. Students can choose to pursue more than one major.

- **Minor.** A secondary area of study, which may or may not be related to the major area of study. Fewer courses are required to fulfill the requirements of a minor. Minors are a way for students to gain knowledge about a subject about which they are passionate or interested, but do not plan to pursue as their primary focus.

- **Office hours.** Dedicated time faculty members set aside on a regular basis for students to ask questions or discuss a course, usually one-on-one.

## The Academic Transition

Just like any new venture in life, your student will make mistakes during their first term of college classes. A successful academic transition takes time and effort. Academic success, just like making new friends, won't just land in your student's lap without significant effort on their part and informed support from you.

One of the biggest academic adjustments for new college students is managing their time. College students have almost all of the responsibility for managing their academic workload and balancing it with other activities and responsibilities. Students are in class fewer hours per day than in high school and must structure their time outside of class to read and complete assignments. Instead of going from class to class all day long, students commonly have a class only two to three days each week, with additional work to complete between meetings.

Unlike in high school, faculty and parents are not there to remind students about upcoming assignments, and students do not have significant time in class to complete work. Some college classes, especially those taken during the first year, are much larger than your student's largest high school class. Faculty members cannot follow up with students to ensure they are on track to complete assignments. This responsibility falls to your student, both to structure their time and to seek help when it's needed. Creating a schedule for the week, including time to socialize and enjoy life, as well as structured time to complete readings and assignments, will help your student adjust to this new academic environment.

College courses are also more rigorous than classes your student took in high school, even if they took many Advanced Placement classes. Increased rigor, combined with the new level of responsibility, means many students struggle or find themselves overwhelmed at some point during the first semester. This is a normal occurrence, though one that is difficult to watch as a parent. One of the first steps to supporting your student is reminding them that bumps in a transition are not unusual.

## Choosing/Changing Majors

Your student may have a dream job or career in mind and may have even shadowed someone in that field. However, college is one of the first true opportunities for them to explore a specific subject or potential career in depth. Encounters with coursework may confirm this vision or cause your student to change their career goals. This is one of the many reasons general education requirements are an important part of the college experience.

There are multiple ways you can support this aspect of your student's academic transition. First, remind them to view their first-year courses through the lens of possibilities, not tasks to check off a list. If they look for general education courses that are even slightly interesting, they may find new interests or even passions. Second, be supportive if your student expresses doubt in their current major, if they have one. A majority of students change their major at least once in college. Tackling this decision on the early side, if possible, is nice, because the later a student decides to change, the more likely they may have to stay for additional time to complete the degree. At some point, your student will have to make a choice and stick with it.

Your student's major or degree does not always equal their lifelong career or even their first job after college. Students often think the major is something they need to know as soon as possible, wanting to draw a line directly from major to career. But much of the learning they do in college, in addition to the content knowledge, is about the mechanics of learning and interacting with people. All three things serve them throughout their post-college life, which often includes work in multiple fields.

Wherever your student is on the spectrum of deciding on a major, from 100% sure to starting college undecided, there are resources on campus to assist. Academic advisors can help connect passions to a degree program and help focus a major or minor. A career center may seem to be something your student doesn't need to think about this early, but it will have resources to help draw connections between areas of study and potential careers. Some students know what they want to study but have no idea what post-college options are available with that degree. Others know what they want to do after college, but do not know what degree options can help get there. Career centers can help with this conversation.

## Overcoming Academic Roadblocks

In moments of an academic struggle, determining the root cause of the issue is important so your student can move forward. This is an excellent opportunity for you to practice letting them drive the conversation. The best way is to ask questions that do not take a yes/no and may not have an obvious answer. Examples include, "What do you think you could do differently in this situation?" and "What campus resources do you think might be available to help with this?" Letting your student find their way through the discomfort and arrive at a solution is good training for future situations in college and beyond.

Every grade and class, especially the first semester or quarter, is a learning experience. This is true whether your student succeeds or struggles. These experiences teach your student about the type of learner they are, what subjects excite them, and where they can anticipate working harder to achieve their academic goals. Even failing or withdrawing from a class midway through the semester (after consulting an academic advisor) is a valuable lesson. Strongly disliking an introductory biology course may cause your student to question their plan to become a doctor, or it may make them work harder because they know biology is important preparation for medical school.

In addition to academic advisors, other immensely helpful resources include tutoring and learning centers, writing centers, faculty office hours, and undergraduate research programs. Even if your student doesn't think they will need any of those services, you can be prepared to nudge them in that direction should the need arise.

Tutoring and learning centers offer help for students in specific subjects, but they also usually offer resources related to academic strategies like time management and test-taking. Staff members may be available to meet with your student about how they learn and how to implement various strategies for academic success. Seeking these resources before students are overwhelmed with a class or multiple classes is important. Writing centers on campus will generally help with writing across all subjects, from English to science lab reports, from brainstorming to structuring a paper to adequately make arguments or cover the expected elements of an assignment. Your student does not need to be struggling to use this resource.

Proactively connecting with faculty, especially in difficult courses and courses in their major, will help your student in those classes as well as develop a better understanding of the field and opportunities available. Instructors typically have time set aside on a weekly basis to meet with students. Of course, your student should meet if they have questions about course content or performance in the class, but they should also meet to get to know the faculty member.

Using these on-campus resources early and proactively is important, before it is a make-or-break situation. And simply expecting common aspects of the transition can also help a student successfully navigate them. For some students, it might work to weave subtle encouragement into conversations before they start college and during the first semester. Others will need overt suggestions to engage with a resource and then report back to you on the experience. You know your student better than anyone else and know what will work. Keeping communication open throughout the transition will help you know when you should suggest investigating these resources.

## Closing Advice

Talk with your student about their academic goals and how they want to be held accountable for achieving them. Do they want you to ask about finding a major each time you talk? Or will they bring it up when they're ready? Communicating up front goes a long way towards productive conversations throughout the next few months.

Being open and supportive, while also knowledgeable about requirements and campus resources, is the best way you can help your student be academically successful. Academic success is about much more than good grades. Success looks different for every student, but includes a mix of enjoyable learning experiences, the identification and pursuit of passions, and yes, grades.

## Conversation Starters

- What parts of the transition to college classes make you nervous or concerned?

- What are your academic goals for the first semester?

- How do you want me to ask about your progress towards your academic goals?

- How will you communicate with me about academic successes, struggles, and grades?

- Do you know how and when your first semester course schedule is created?

## Chapter 5
# WHAT WILL THIS COST, AND WHO'S PAYING?

How to navigate the bill and financial decisions

**Benjamin M. Williams**
**Georgia State**

There are many different approaches to financing your student's education. Some families have been saving for years and can contribute greatly to expenses. In other situations, the student will be fully responsible for funding their education. You likely have many questions at this point:

- Where will the money for the bill come from each semester?

- Who has to pay back these loans, and when?

- How much will textbooks and supplies cost?

- Will my student be able to find a campus job to help with some expenses?

- How many times a week do they really need to order pizza when we're paying for a meal plan?

Navigating the financial side of higher education is an important and complicated process at times. The who, what, and how of college finances is the focus of this chapter.

## Common Financial Terms

- **FAFSA.** The Free Application for Student Aid (FAFSA) is the way that the Department of Education will determine student eligibility for federal aid. This document is submitted by the student, using tax information from the family. There is no fee to submit this application and it must be submitted each year.

- **Federal student loans.** There are several types of federal loans and it is important to know the differences.

  - **Subsidized federal loans:** The interest is paid by the Department of Education during the student's time in school. These are the loans that should be taken first if available.

  - **Unsubsidized federal loans:** The interest is accrued while the student is in school.

  - **Parent PLUS loans:** A parent can apply for this loan, which is the parent's responsibility but paid to the student's account directly. It is based on credit. If you aren't approved, additional loans will be made available to your student.

- **Private student loans.** If your student is not granted enough federal aid, private loans can help cover that gap. Unlike federal loans, private loan terms will depend on the borrower's credit.

- **Grants, scholarships, and Work-Study.** There are a variety of financing options that don't require you or your student to pay money back.

  ○ **Grants:** Federal grants like the Pell Grant or institutional grants do not require payment. They are often income-based.

  ○ **Scholarships:** Eligibility for institutional scholarships will occur at application. Some schools also have scholarship listings and support to help locate outside scholarships, and your student can also research external scholarships on their own.

  ○ **Work-Study:** This is a federal program, associated with income requirements, that cannot be applied to tuition, but can provide a paycheck during studies.

- **Expected Family Contribution (EFC).** The EFC is a metric used by the federal government to determine the financial ability of families to contribute to college. A student can borrow loans up to the total cost of attendance, but the EFC will impact eligibility for Pell Grants and other scholarships. This is not an amount you are expected to pay, but is what the Department of Education believes you could.

- **Cost of attendance (COA).** This is the amount that is determined to be the cost of attending a particular university or college. COA varies by institution and is determined by various factors. For instance, the housing cost will be different if the institution is in a large city versus a rural area.

- **Refund.** A refund is a payment to the student of any excess financial aid (loans, grants, scholarships) over the COA that is sent to a bank account put on file by the student. This can be used to pay for an off-campus apartment and other expenses.

## Conversations about Money

Who will fund college is a top-of-mind issue, particularly as you receive the college's financial package and the due date for the first payment approaches. There is no wrong way to support your student, but don't avoid the conversation. The sooner you discuss numbers and expectations, the better. Everyone needs to understand what they will contribute and the value of education.

Remember that finances should be an ongoing conversation. You may want to plan for a monthly financial check-in to make sure your student's budget is on track, or at least bring it up semesterly when it comes time to pay the bill. However often you decide to bring up money, being honest and forthcoming in these conversations makes it easier on everyone and will eliminate issues later on. You don't want to get a call that your student has already spent their summer job earnings by October.

To prepare to have financial conversations with your student, here are some questions to consider:

- *How much will you contribute?* The first element will be deciding how much you, as a parent, can contribute to tuition, fees, and housing. While loans and scholarships may cover the bulk, the need for additional funds is likely. You should be honest and direct with your student about how much you will contribute.

- *How much will your student contribute?* The other key part of the equation is your student's role, and their ability to make money through work. While you may have some concerns about your student balancing academics and a job, studies have shown that students who work are better able to keep a schedule and, in turn, do better in school. There are particular benefits to working on campus, where the focus will still be on education. Setting clear expectations around hours, benefits of an on- or off-campus job, budgets, and what happens if grades start to fall are important to discuss proactively.

- *Who will pay for extras?* Textbooks, school supplies, club fees, tickets to sporting events, laundry, gas, and entertainment: think about where you will support your student with these extra expenses and what they will have to fund themselves.

- *What expenses should go into your student's budget?* Perhaps your student has never kept a formal budget. Perhaps you haven't either! Now is the perfect time to get your student started with the good habit of keeping a budget, whether it is built from savings and summer job income or weekly paycheck from their campus job.

- *How will we talk about money?* If your student runs out of funds or finds themselves in a financial bind, can they call you? How will you hold them accountable to the budget created? Support without encouraging bad habits is key in this area. This is a great time for your student to learn how to effectively manage their money. If you jump in to save them every time they mismanage it, they will miss some important learning opportunities. Setting expectations in advance will help them navigate money management.

## Putting the Pieces Together

There are a variety of ways to fund education, and ultimately it is about putting the pieces together in a way that makes sense to your family. The key components will be bringing together a combination of the bill due, the aid awarded, and what is available to fill in the gaps. It is critical that between any support you can provide and the aid available, you should, at a minimum, match the cost of attendance. The goal is to not take on excess debt.

If you are ever in doubt or feel lost, there are resources available. One of the best places to check for information will always be the institution's website. Each institution is different, but will help support your student as they prepare to enroll. Some key offices to look for are:

| | |
|---|---|
| **Student accounts or bursar** | The office that processes payments for tuition and fees is called student accounts, the bursar, or the cashier's office. |
| **Office of financial aid** | The office that oversees the processing of FAFSA and the awarding of financial aid is often called financial aid or student financial management centers. |
| **Scholarship office** | The office that assists with scholarships is often called the scholarship office or scholarship resource center. This office may be combined with the financial aid office. |

An additional resource, if the campus provides one, is the parent and family programs office. These are campus-based professionals who are focused on supporting you and can assist in answering your questions or helping you find resources. The admissions office will also have information about aid and financial support.

## Closing Advice

The cost of college can feel scary. With the media talking about ballooning costs and student debt, it is understandable that there is anxiety as you plan for your student's enrollment. Understanding all available resources, setting expectations early, and having clear communication with your student about money will help set you up for success.

## Conversation Starters

- What kind of campus jobs will you be applying for?

- How will you balance working with your academics?

- What expenses do you anticipate having outside of academic/housing expenses?

- How do you plan to cover your expenses while at college?

- How will you keep track of your money?

- Do you want to set a budget for the week or for the month?

- Do you know the difference between a credit and debit card?

# Chapter 6
# HOW CAN I HELP MY STUDENT STAY HEALTHY?

How to prepare for physical and mental wellness

**Lady Cox**
**Auburn University**

In addition to challenging your student's mind, the transition to college will challenge their body. Everything that affects their health is about to change: the food they eat, the way in which they get exercise, the bed on which they sleep, the schedule they keep, and more. These changes in lifestyle can affect weight, skin, and mood. Preparing for these changes now can help prevent negative effects later.

## A Healthy Start

There will be many tasks to complete the summer before your student starts college. In between buying bedding and registering for classes, it's important to focus on your student's physical health as well. Medical appointments and exams during the summer can give you peace of mind that your student is healthy when they head to school.

The most critical medical appointment for your student is for their immunizations. Most colleges have a list of immunizations that must be completed prior to starting classes. The documentation of these immunizations can be difficult to assemble, so it is best to start early.

The summer is the best time for your student to see all of their clinicians for a last checkup, especially if they have any ongoing treatments or daily medications. They should meet with their primary clinician, dentist, allergist, gynecologist, optometrist, psychologist, or psychiatrist. If your student is traveling far from home, they should use these appointments to talk with their clinicians about a treatment plan while they are away at school. Your student should also get copies of their prescriptions, referrals to clinicians in their new college town (if needed), and appointments for when they return home.

One of the best parts of these visits is allowing your student to see that they are now in charge of their own medical care. They will, hopefully, be comfortable with their existing clinicians to talk about health, treatment, and next steps. Talk to your student in advance of these appointments and prepare them for the conversations. Allow them to do the visit alone. If you must be in the room, try to stay silent and let your student ask their own questions. Afterwards, talk through how they might prepare for conversations with a new clinician. Remind them that it can be uncomfortable for anyone to discuss their bodies, emotions, and needs, but they should trust their doctor and be honest about what they are experiencing.

## Student Health Center

Most colleges have a student health center on campus that offers a convenient way for students to see a clinician. At some universities, students pay a fee so that they can see a clinician without an additional charge. Others have a fee-for-service model, which means your student will be responsible for a copay or deductible, with insurance covering the remainder. Learn the specifics of your student's campus so you can help them know what to expect.

Many college students need to have frequent medical appointments for allergy shots, hormone injections, blood tests, or other treatments. The university health center should be familiar with these needs, as they are very common. During the summer, research what is needed to transfer the treatment protocol from your home clinician to the clinic on campus or a local provider. This same advice applies to students with chronic health conditions. Students with any long-term medical condition should reach out to the student clinic to discuss medical history and current treatment, and to create a relationship so that if they fall ill, the clinic will be better equipped to treat them.

One of the most important steps is to determine if your health insurance will cover your student at their school's health center and in the community. If your insurance is not accepted, or if you do not have insurance, research the university's insurance plan.

You also need to identify a pharmacy for your student to use while in college. This service may be provided by the university's health center, or you may choose to use a national pharmacy that has a location near campus. If your student has frequent prescription medication needs, it is best to go ahead and transfer their prescriptions to the pharmacy before the semester begins so it will be handled once they are on campus.

## Access to Student Medical Records

One of the hardest transitions for parents as their students enter college is lack of access to records. You should expect that your student's medical records will be protected and that their medical clinicians will not talk to you about the care they are receiving. Medical records are governed by HIPAA and have many confidentiality requirements.

You may hear new college parents discussing the need for a power of attorney for their student with the belief that, if your student is incapcitated, this is the only way that parents can make decisions. The truth is that this is unnecessary and costly. Your student's college will have a way for them to set up an emergency contact. In an emergency where a student is incapacitated, family will be consulted as next of kin, regardless of whether or not you have created a power of attorney.

## Support for Specialized Needs

Some students have unique needs that require specialized attention to ensure the transition to college goes smoothly. Students with ADD, ADHD, dyslexia, or other learning differences should have access to accommodations to support them in their courses. Students with dietary restrictions or chronic health concerns should make plans in advance to keep themselves as safe as possible. Whatever additional support your student needs, take comfort in knowing that there is no other time in their life where there will be so many professionals dedicated to ensuring that they succeed.

Most colleges have an office to support students with disabilities. To qualify for accommodations, students must provide medical documentation of their disability status and their needs while on campus. These accommodations assist students with disabilities to learn the same material and meet the same academic standards as their peers. The critical thing to note about requesting accommodations is that it is best to do so as early as possible, and certainly before classes begin. This is especially important for housing accommodations that need to be made early enough to ensure the needed type of housing is available.

## Dietary Restrictions

Dietary restrictions are a concern for a growing number of college students. While some allergies can be easily accommodated, others require students to make requests in advance. If the college has a required meal plan that appears to be difficult to use with the available dining venues, contact the dining office to see what other options are available.

## Physical Health

For your student to perform well academically, they need to stay strong physically. This means eating healthy food, getting plenty of exercise, and sleeping enough. While all colleges strive to provide healthy dining options for students, if your student wants to eat only french fries and chicken fingers, they will be able to do so.

One way you can help your student to make healthy food choices is by talking to them about how different types of food affect a person's body and performance. When they call home and talk to you about how they feel physically, talk through what they have been eating. It might be tempting to send your student care packages of sweets. Instead, try to find a grocery delivery service that will deliver healthy, prepared meals they can heat up in the microwave.

Exercise is also an essential part of staying strong. In addition to access to a gym, encourage your student to check out intramural sports teams, outdoor adventure sports, group fitness classes, and so on. There is no better time than college to try out brand new activities. Remind your student that, in addition to the health benefits, participating in these activities is also an opportunity to meet new friends.

The last thing to remember about staying strong is the importance of sleep. Your student still needs roughly eight hours a night of restful sleep. It is common for college students to stay up later than they did in high school. Have them pack an eye mask and ear plugs made for sleep in case their roommate has a different schedule.

## Mental Health

Perhaps nothing worries parents more about the transition to college than wondering if their student will be okay emotionally. Everything in your student's life is about to change, and there is a legitimate concern that this will affect their mental health. When it comes to your student, remember that you are the expert and you should trust your gut. If you think your student needs additional support, you are probably right.

Your student's campus will have mental health professionals focused on helping college students succeed and who are very familiar with the types of issues students face. Most universities offer these services at no charge to students. If your student already regularly meets with a mental health care provider, it is best to talk through how to make the transition to college. Some counselors may want to continue sessions using telehealth options, while others may suggest your student transition to a local practitioner once they arrive on campus.

The goal of counseling is to improve your student's psychological well-being. Regardless of what challenge your student is facing (e.g., homesickness, end of romantic relationship, questioning sexuality), a psychologist or counselor is there to help them talk through their experience and create a plan for moving forward.

As your student gains independence, they may also choose to make changes to their health care on their own. It's not uncommon for students to decide they want to stop taking their medications or seeing a psychologist once they are in college. It is difficult to watch your student make decisions that are different from your own, but these are opportunities for them to learn as well. Try to support your student in this exploration, but remind them of the resources available.

## Closing Advice

There are so many different aspects to health and wellness that supporting your student in this way may seem daunting. Remember to take it one appointment and conversation at a time, and that many issues may not arise until later. Be prepared by understanding the resources and knowing how your student handles illness and stress. Encourage healthy behaviors since a balanced lifestyle can make all the difference in your student's success.

---

### Conversation Starters

- Do you know what questions to ask the doctor at your next appointment?
- Who have you put down as your emergency contact?
- How will you know when you're feeling stressed, and what steps will you take?
- How will you stay active on campus?
- Have you talked to your roommate about sleeping patterns and schedules?

---

## Chapter 7
# WHAT IF MY STUDENT WILL BE LIVING AT HOME?

How to support commuter and remote students

**Andrea Mitchen**
**University of Houston**

In the year(s) of COVID-19, many new college students experienced a new way of learning that commuter students have known for years: living with their families while transitioning to a new phase of life. This year has definitely presented an unexpected challenge for those not inclined to reside in their family homes, but rest assured: there are methods of creating an environment that is conducive to learning and meets the needs of both student and family.

As a parent of a commuter student, you may think that your home dynamic will not change much as your student embarks on this college journey, but it will. Sometimes this will be in ways that you can expect, perhaps even attempt to control, but things will undoubtedly change. Creating, revisiting, and maintaining expectations and boundaries is the key to a successful transition.

Students live with their parents and families for multiple reasons. It can be a financial decision, a family responsibility, or a cultural tradition, but respecting each other and growing together will vastly improve your student's experience in this new phase of life.

## Prepare for Change

When students enter their college residence halls, there is an expectation from staff that they have developed (or will soon develop) what we consider basic life skills, such as doing laundry, maintaining a budget, and creating a healthy place to live and study. But what do you do when your student resides in their childhood bedroom, sits at your dining table, and steals the remote control to watch their favorite teenage drama? Do you allow things to stay exactly the same or do you embrace the notion that your student is different than they were in high school?

Here are some questions to consider early on:

- Have you discussed your student's schedule and how often they will be on campus for class and studying?
- How will your student get to and from campus?
- Will chores at home still be required?
- Is your student responsible for the care of family members in the home and have you talked about balancing that responsibility with their new academic schedule?
- How will you encourage your student to stay on campus for involvement opportunities, study sessions, and use of campus resources?

You will want to think about how you can make it easier for your student to switch back and forth between life at home and on campus. For example, does your student's college have a commuter meal plan, or another way of depositing funds that will make it easier to find lunch/snacks while on campus? If they will have a job, will it be more convenient for them to work on campus or near home? Do they have the right backpack or bag to carry all of the materials needed for their days on campus, or can they rent a locker?

Parents whose students move into campus housing celebrate this transition throughout the summer in little ways, like shopping for dorm necessities and having goodbye dinners with grandparents and close friends. You too should celebrate your student's transition into college, even if it looks a little different. Maybe it's time to redecorate or refurnish their childhood bedroom to give it a college feel. If they will be driving, make a big deal out of getting the oil changed and the car inspected, and spend time teaching them how to do these things themselves. Even though they aren't leaving the family home, throw an "off to college" party prior to the first day of classes. Ask about course schedules, orientation plans, ideas to join a club, and other things that will make your student excited about starting a new academic adventure.

## Plan the Commute

As you can imagine, when considering a commuter student's schedule there are more factors than just class time. When they map out their day, they have to consider commute times, time/distance from parking lot to class, class times, study time, etc. You can support your new commuter student by asking them to consider all of these things in a daily schedule, planner, or other agenda method that has assisted with time management in the past.

Ask if your student has considered how they will use the commute time. If they choose public transit, they could study on the way to campus. If in the car, perhaps they would like to listen to recorded notes. Carpooling with friends could be a way to get a study session in. Or your student may choose to use this time to destress with their favorite podcast, audio book, or musical selection. Taking time for yourself is never wasted, as decompression often can produce productivity later on.

If a student chooses to drive their personal vehicle, they will need to consider the cost of parking on campus and obtain a parking permit to do so. If you live in a place where public transit is an option, your student might need to inquire about campus/local transit discounts for students and how they work. Sometimes the only option is to share a family vehicle or be transported by a family member to campus. If this is the case, how can you ensure that your student has time to not only go to class, but be a college student and participate in campus activities?

## Discuss Household Contributions

When your student was in primary and secondary school, they were responsible for contributing to your household in many ways. Will chores and caring for others around the house still be expected? A serious conversation about expectations in the home should happen prior to the first day of class.

Many families have multiple children and/or generations living under one roof. Who will now pick up little brother from baseball practice or little sister from choir? Consider how those responsibilities might need to change and shift. Helping your student develop a new routine will be very important for their success in the transition to commuting college student.

## Connect to the Campus Community

There is plenty of scholarly evidence and research that supports the importance of student involvement and its relationship to success, belonging, and connection to campus. This is even more important for a commuter student. Students who commute are generally less likely to feel connected to campus and less informed about campus resources and services, but it does not have to be that way. There are multiple ways for commuter students to be engaged, and things you can do to encourage this engagement:

- Make sure they read their email. Many universities send regular postings (usually through a "weekly happenings" email) about upcoming events and involvement opportunities. Your student might not love email, but it is the primary way universities communicate with students.

- Encourage them to visit the campus events calendar regularly. Some colleges and universities even have the option of adding these events to students' own personal calendars.

- Suggest that they study, eat, work out, and spend time on campus. It is easy for a commuter student to study alone in their room, go home to eat if it is within a reasonable radius, and work out at their local gym. All of these spaces typically exist on college campuses and it is often the informal and unplanned interactions that can change a student's feelings about their college experience. Student fees fund a lot of the services and facilities that commuter students might forget to use. Help your student get the most from their (your) money!

- Most important: teach, encourage, and beg your student to stay on campus beyond class time. This helps commuter students become aware of what's going on on campus and to get engaged.

## Consider Family Relationships

When a student moves away for college, changes in their values, communication styles and frequency, and personality are very evident to the parent who only sees them on occasion. While these changes will feel more subtle to the family that is living with their college student, they will still happen. This may be most evident in the way you communicate as your student becomes more engaged in college life. Your check-ins may shift to texts rather than hallway chats. You might notice your student brings up new, and perhaps controversial for your family, topics of conversation at the dinner table. Or maybe when you overhear their discussions in a virtual class or group assignment, you find that they act very differently than they do with their family. Remember that your student is trying to juggle home life with the person they are away from home, just like you do when you work and come home. This may be difficult to see and negotiate at first and may cause some stress for your family. Remember that these transitions are completely normal for all college students; enjoy watching them shift into the adult they are becoming!

## Closing Advice

Even if your student will be learning at home or commuting, they are still going through a significant transition and need your support. While you may have expectations for them at home, recognize that they need to be present on campus and have time to focus on academics and college life. Help them understand how to balance and what resources are available, and encourage their independence.

### Conversation Starters

- How do you feel about commuting to campus?
- Have you been to campus to see where to park and where your first class is?
- Who will you call if your primary source of commuting is unavailable?
- How can I help you be involved on campus?
- How can I help you have the time at school needed to get the experience you want?

Chapter 8
# IS MY STUDENT READY TO ADULT?

## How to prepare your student for college responsibilities

**Kristin Austin**
**West Chester University of PA**

It's the little things: coming behind your teen after they've left for school to make sure they unplugged their straightener. And the big things: reviewing how to change a flat tire…on the side of the road… in the dark…in the middle of a downpour. It's the rites of passage lovingly referred to as "adulting." Adulting is the range of behaviors, attitudes, and habits generally expected of late adolescence and early adulthood, which is also when your student might be leaving the nest for college or flying nest-adjacent as a commuter student.

Because parents often spend the K–12 years checking the lists, making the calls, and signing the forms, it can be a bit jarring once a student begins college. How does one aptly sum all the tips, steps, reminders, and "in the event of…" knowledge that has been curated so carefully over 18 years that it's now reflex?

The truth is, you can't. Adulting is a combination of sink, swim, and tread, and the college transition is the pool in which it all happens. In this chapter, we will explore some new experiences college can bring and how you can help your student swim and minimize the moments of flailing around and sinking.

## Safety on Campus

Starting college can sometimes feel like an all-inclusive vacation. The suitcase has been rolled down the runway, the energy is high, there are unlimited sights to explore, and the amenities are alluring. However, just like vacationing in any new environment, in addition to enjoying the beauty and fun, it is important to know the policies, risks, strategies for responsibility, local laws, and your own safety plan.

### Campus Security

Most colleges have some form of a policing or safety department located on the campus. Your student should know the exact location of the department and should program the phone number of the department into their phone. For some campuses, calling 911 is slower than calling the campus police or safety department.

Does your student's new campus have a safety app? If so, encourage them to download it before they arrive on campus. Campus-based apps often offer enhanced tracking features that are specially designed for the campus geography, allowing for more pinpointed location tracking, such as that corner study room on the 10th floor of the library that otherwise has terrible service. Exploring the app together over the summer allows you to use it as a springboard to discuss safety topics.

Most campuses have some version of an emergency alert system, which can consist of text messages, phone calls, emails, and possibly loudspeaker announcements. Campuses use these alerts sparingly and only in the case of true emergencies. Your student should regularly verify that the college has their correct phone number on file to guarantee they will receive emergency alerts. Remind your student to also verify emergency contact information on file, which allows the university to quickly reach you if necessary.

Colleges, no matter how big or small, urban or rural, private or public, all experience crime. It's important to absorb this message because some students—and their families—can have a romanticized view of a crime-free bubble, based on the college website and brochure. Colleges are small or large communities that are much like the cities, townships, or counties you come from. There are people from all walks of life, with all different experiences. Like the world, overwhelmingly most students are good citizens. However, some are not. This is why a conversation about personal safety is so important.

Even schools with the most pristine reputation experience the same crimes that exist outside of the campus boundaries: theft, assault, underage substance use, sale of illegal merchandise, fraud, and worse. As a result, campuses nationwide unanimously recommend personal responsibility practices as the first deterrent to crime.

## Physical Safety

When it comes to physical safety, non-lethal personal protection includes alarms/whistles, pepper spray, stun guns, and keychain weapons. Before investing in any of these items, check with the policies of your campus to learn what is and is not permitted on campus, including firearms (a permit does not mean it will be allowed on campus). Many campuses offer self-defense workshops and classes. Bonus if the classes count for college credit!

## Property Safety

The most common crime on college campuses tends to be petty theft. It is very important that students are frequently reminded to lock their dorms/apartments, lock bikes with a sturdy U-lock, and never leave belongings unattended in the library, dining hall, or other public spaces where theft can easily occur. Students can bring a small safe for important items, or may choose to engrave electronics for easy identification. A surprising theft? Textbooks. Make sure your student keeps an eye on their books.

## Identity Safety

Theft is not just physical; it can also be virtual. Theft of virtual property, such as identity, is a critical conversation to have in preparation for adulthood. Because of the technological milieu in which Generation Z was raised, most students have grown up with the message of online safety as it relates to predators, but possibly less messaging that relates to identity theft. College-age individuals can be susceptible to identify theft or fraud as they seek to establish a credit history and begin using social media for professional networking. For this reason, students should be encouraged to keep their passwords safely secured, and not to be shared with anyone, including parents. Now might also be a good time to invest in a credit monitoring service for your student so they can be alerted of any suspected fraudulent activity.

## Personal Responsibility

### Vehicle Responsibility

If your student has a car, automobile care is an important part of adulthood. Basic maintenance such as tire pressure and oil health are important life skills. Whether you choose to empower your student by teaching them car maintenance, or by simply equipping them with a 24/7 roadside assistance membership, your student needs to know what to do if they encounter a car emergency.

Student drivers, including those who are commuters, should have a trunk stocked with general safety supplies, such as a first aid kit; weather supplies, such as a shovel and rock salt; a blanket; flashlight; spare tire; jumper cables; and flare lights. If the student is parking on campus, make sure they know the parking regulations of the campus and city, such as ticketing, towing, and parking schedules. The last thing you want your student to come home with is a semester's worth of parking tickets!

## Cooking

Families might assume tasks such as cooking, laundry, and cleaning aren't things that need to be taught. However, every university professional has a story about a student who didn't remove the pizza from the cardboard box before putting in the oven or who didn't add water to the ramen before microwaving. The quickest way for a new student to gain unwanted attention is to be the person that burns popcorn in a residence hall. With a few lessons, students can be prepared for these personal responsibilities.

Familiarize your student with the appliances their campus allows. Most colleges have stringent restrictions on what appliances can exist in a residence hall due to fire hazards and power amperage concerns. Even just a fridge and microwave equips a student to make quick meals. When discussing how to properly use appliances, begin by asking your student how they would currently use the appliance while still living at home. You may find they are using it very well already, or entirely wrong. Now is the time to find this out, not at 2 a.m. when they have set off the smoke alarms in a building of 500 students. Remember to remind them to always check that they turned off the stove or oven…twice, to be safe.

## Cleanliness

Whether sharing 230 square feet of living space with a roommate or enjoying the freedom of a sprawling mansion, contributing to the cleanliness of one's personal and shared spaces is expected. To prepare your student for cleaning, consider equipping them with a basic chore kit that includes neutral cleaning substances. If you choose to provide supplies that are surface-specific, educate them on the correct usage of each product on each surface, as well as the dangers of using the products incorrectly, especially if the product could damage university property. Encourage your student to have a conversation with their roommate(s) about any scent or chemical sensitivities in advance. Finally, equip your student with a general cleaning calendar that outlines how often certain areas or items should be cleaned (dishes, every day; sheets, every week or every other week).

## Laundry

Speaking of laundry, while immaculate laundry neatly folded in drawers and hanging in the closet might be a fantasy, we can at the very least, get students to a point where any clothing strewn about the room is clean. To prepare for college laundering, explain the settings on washing and drying machines. Although the units used on campus may be different from what you have at home, understanding basic settings can go a long way. Your student needs to know what can and can't be washed together and how many items constitute a full load. Loads in which the colors have bled or a shirt has shrunk by two sizes is often a rite of passage for new students. With a little education, though, you can extend the life of the clothing and possibly lessen how much laundry your student brings home—double win!

## Diversity & Inclusion

Peer relationships are one of the most important topics to discuss when entering adulthood. Your student is sure to encounter new diversities in college that they haven't previously been familiar with. The diversity of race, religion, gender expression, sexuality, personal values—among many other characteristics—that students will experience can be shocking to their sense of familiarity and comfort. In most cases, students have not shared a room, or a hall, or a house with someone of an entirely different religion, ethnicity, or ability status. This new experience offers a wealth of opportunities for both parties to learn and grow, but it can also bring about feelings of uncertainty or fear.

While you can never be fully prepared for what it will be like to live with a complete stranger, you can prepare your student with ideas on how to confront their implicit bias, how to have inclusive, respectful interactions, and how to be open-minded. Engaging in discussions around difference before your student begins college will help prepare them to contribute to a positive and inclusive campus climate for all. If you are unsure of how to support your student in this area, contact the student affairs department of the university and ask for appropriate resources. Diversity and inclusion are great topics to explore as a family!

## Closing Advice

It's not too late to make sure your student is prepared for adult responsibilities in college. Take time over the summer to cover these topics, and remember that none are "one and done" conversations. It will take some mistakes along the way—along with some tips and reminders from you—before your student is 100% ready to "adult."

## Conversation Starters

- Have you downloaded your school's safety app?
- Do you know how to change a tire?
- Do you know how much laundry detergent to use?
- How often should you be washing your sheets and towels?
- How can you balance a diet of chicken fingers with healthy options?

## Chapter 9
# HOW CAN I SAY THIS...?

## How to initiate difficult conversations

**Christine Self**
**Texas Tech University**

Alcohol, drugs, sex, and relationships: these are all difficult topics to discuss. Your student's upcoming departure to college is a reminder that soon they will be on their own and you will no longer be able to monitor their behavior and initiate conversations when you notice something is up. This summer is a time to revisit these conversations in the context of college life.

The purpose of this chapter is not to challenge your family's values about these topics, but to provide you with tools and tips to prepare you to have tough discussions with your student. How and when to have these conversations will look different for every family. Talk with your student about these topics bit by bit. Don't try to cover everything at once in a marathon session. Talk while having a meal with your student, or when they are driving and you're in the passenger seat so they can't tune you out by scrolling on their phone. Plan a weekly lunch with just you and your student at a quiet spot or use the drive to talk. It may seem awkward, but these are important conversations you won't want to skip. Take a deep breath....

## Alcohol

Whether you believe that drinking alcohol is simply a reality of college life, or you strongly feel that underage drinking is illegal for a reason and your student should never engage in it, there are important things to know about college students and alcohol use.

### The facts

Studies have shown that up to 40% of college students 18 and older said they used alcohol weekly.

### Conversations to have about alcohol use

First, share your family's values regarding alcohol. Talk about your expectations about your student's alcohol use, whether this is total abstinence from alcohol until age 21 or drinking in moderation and never drinking and driving. Talk specifically and openly about your values and expectations. It is important not to simply tell your student not to drink and leave it at that. Avoid shutting the door for future conversations about alcohol by telling your student that, if they have questions or concerns about their peers' or their own experiences with alcohol, that you are here to listen. Find out what your student's school's policies are regarding alcohol consumption. Since these policies and regulations don't come from you—they come from your student's college—having this discussion from that angle may be an easier place to begin.

Drinking and driving is never safe. They should always have a backup plan, whether it's a safe ride program, Uber or Lyft, or a sober friend to call. Encourage your student to have apps and payment methods updated and/or check with a friend who plans to be sober before engaging in drinking away from their own room or apartment.

Discuss the warning signs of alcohol poisoning with your student. These include mental confusion, unresponsiveness, gasping for air, throwing up, clammy skin, erratic breathing, loss of consciousness, and paleness of skin. Many colleges and universities have amnesty clauses in their codes of student conduct so that students can seek help from university staff (like residence hall employees) if their roommate or a friend needs help without fear of getting in trouble for drinking.

Binge drinking, defined as consuming five or more drinks in about two hours for men and four or more drinks in about two hours for women, is another important topic to discuss. Talk about the effects of binge drinking on one's performance as a college student and on one's health. Ask your student to think about their goals for being in college in the first place. Will being hungover all weekend help them achieve those goals? Being unable to focus on assignments, student organization obligations, and other important activities will interfere with their classes, relationships, and overall well-being.

## Drugs

Talking about drug use can be tricky. Generational differences about the acceptance of drugs such as marijuana, especially in states where the drug is legal, can cause strife.

### The facts

About 20% of college students reported using marijuana in the last 30 days.

### Conversations to have about drug use

Once again, talk openly and specifically about your family's values surrounding drug use and share your expectations about your student's behavior. Leave the door open for your student to come to you for help if they have concerns about their or their peers' drug use.

Remind them that, even though you hope they will not use illegal drugs or violate their college's policies, that you are there to help them find assistance if they do. Avoid coming across as judgmental or laughing off discussions about drugs (or alcohol, for that matter).

Make sure you are aware of college policies and local and state laws regarding drug use and discuss these with your student. Review your student's school's resources for drug education as well as policies related to drug use on campus. In a growing number of states, once your student turns 21, they can legally possess and consume marijuana, so familiarize yourself with state laws where they will be studying.

## Sex and Relationships

Talking about safer sex, sexual violence and consent, and healthy intimate relationships may be the most challenging conversation yet. Students are more likely to come to their parents for advice and help if something goes wrong if they have had open, honest conversations with them about these topics.

### The facts

33% of college students said they had sexual intercourse within the past two weeks.

### Conversations to have about sex and relationships

Talk about your family's values. If your values include abstinence from sex prior to marriage, share that with your student, but instead of simply saying, "no sex before marriage," tell them that, though you would prefer they not engage in premarital sex, if they do decide to have sex, they should protect themselves from sexually transmitted infections and unplanned pregnancies by using condoms and birth control. Find out where they will be able to find condoms on campus. They are often available for free at the student health office or from RAs, for example.

Make sure you discuss sexual consent with your student—both how to get consent and how to give consent. Your student's college will have a policy about consent in its code of student conduct; this would be an excellent place to start. Remind them that consent is an ongoing process and someone must get consent for sexual activity every time. Just because there was consent for sex on Friday night does not mean there is consent for sex on Saturday morning. If you are unsure of how to begin, search for ideas on YouTube or Google that can serve as conversation starters or to help you develop your own talking points.

In conversations about sexual violence, avoid inadvertently placing blame on anyone but the perpetrator. For example, messages about not dressing in revealing clothing to avoid assault tell students that they would be to blame if they were assaulted while dressed in certain ways. This might inhibit them from reporting assault to authorities (or to their parents).

Sexual violence is never the victim's fault, regardless of alcohol consumption. But since alcohol is a factor in many instances of sexual violence on college campuses, talk to your student about having a plan if they become incapacitated by alcohol, having a plan if their partner (or potential partner) is incapacitated, and being a good bystander for peers who become incapacitated. Good conversation starters might include:

- What would you do if you went to a party and found you were getting drunk?

- What would you do if you realized a person you were interested in being intimate with was incapacitated by alcohol?

- What would you do if a friend you went to a party with was drunk and in a vulnerable position?

Talk to your student about what a healthy intimate relationship looks like. If you are in a healthy relationship, talk to your student about what makes your relationship successful and beneficial to you and your partner. Signs of a healthy relationship include moving at a comfortable pace, honesty, respect, kindness, healthy conflict, trust, independence, equality, taking responsibility, and having fun.

On the other side of the coin, warning signs of an unhealthy relationship include overly intense feelings and over-the-top behaviors, manipulation, sabotage of other relationships or reputation, possessiveness, isolation from other peers and family members, belittling, and volatility. If your student is in a serious relationship, ask them how things are going. If you notice any red flags or any of the signs listed above in your student's relationship, tell them you are there to support them if they need help.

Avoid putting pressure on your student to date before they are ready. It's okay if your student hasn't yet dipped their toes into the dating waters. You may have met your significant other during your college years, but students today often wait until later in life to seek serious dating relationships. Though it may seem natural to you to reminisce about dating in college, too much of this in your conversations inadvertently pressure your student into feeling their single status is abnormal or that they cannot live up to your expectations of college life.

Encourage your student to reach out for help on campus if they need it. Even if your student does not want to file a formal complaint, the Title IX office on campus can assist with supportive measures such as moving residence halls, parking lots, or even altering class schedules in the cases of interpersonal violence, sexual harassment, stalking, or sexual violence.

## Finding Extra Support

You may have identified other important topics to discuss with your student based on their specific needs. Students may come to college with specific mental health challenges, such as anxiety, depression, or eating disorders. The great news is that colleges and universities are more equipped than ever to help support students' success as they navigate these issues. Familiarize yourself with the resources your student's school has to offer through its counseling center or other departments. Talk to your student about these resources and ask about their plan if they feel anxious, depressed, or need extra support. Will they call or text you? Check in with the counseling center? Join a student support group? It's important for them to formulate a plan and share it with you. You can start these conversations using the prompts in this book.

## Closing Advice

Though alcohol, drugs, and sex and relationships are difficult conversations to have with anyone, let alone as a parent or family member supporting a college student, they are crucial. Students look to their families for role modeling and support, even if it often seems like your words might be going in one ear and out the other. You know your student better than anyone, and your words and advice are important to them.

## Conversation Starters

- What are your college's policies about alcohol and drug use?

- What will you do if you're at a party and find you cannot drive home?

- How will you say no to a peer if you are not interested in consuming alcohol or drugs?

- What values would you like to see in an intimate partner?

- How do you get sexual consent? How do you give sexual consent?

# Chapter 10
# HOW MUCH STUFF WILL FIT IN A DORM ROOM?

## How to pack and prepare for college life

### Stephanie Stiltner
### University of Pikeville

The short answer to the question, "How much stuff will fit in a dorm room?" is: not as much as you think. As a matter of fact, it's not uncommon for families to leave campus on move-in day with items that didn't fit into their student's new living space.

Shopping for college will be surprisingly similar to the back-to-school shopping trips from your past. The biggest differences are you'll be purchasing laundry baskets and mattress pads instead of crayons and safety scissors and your student is in charge this time. This shopping experience will hopefully also come with fewer meltdowns in the backpack aisle.

The first place your student should visit is the housing and/or residence life page on their college's website. The information provided by this office is your student's guide to preparing to live on campus.

## Living Experience in the Residence Hall

Living in a residence hall is a unique experience. Inhabiting a tight space will be an especially huge transition if your student has always had their own room, but even those who have shared a room may feel differently about being in such close quarters with a stranger. Sharing a bathroom with your family is very different from sharing a bathroom with dozens of people. Rolling out of bed for breakfast isn't the same when you have to walk outside to get to the dining hall.

When shopping for college, encourage your student to think about how they will live, prepare food, sleep, get dressed, study, and socialize in their new space. Be creative with storage; deploy under-bed space by using plastic bins or drawers if possible. Encourage your student to choose decorations that reflect their personality and make their space feel like a home away from home.

Remember that your student and their roommate might have different schedules, and it's important to make sound sleep a priority. Consider a sound machine or white noise app, a fan to keep the room cool and comfortable, a mattress topper for comfort, a sleep mask to block light, and noise-canceling headphones or earplugs.

Encourage your student to connect with their roommate and discuss who will bring which of the bigger items (e.g., TV, fridge). Not only is it unnecessary to have multiples of these items, but there likely won't be space.

## Pack Only What They'll Need

Have you ever packed for vacation and tossed outfits into your suitcase just in case you needed them, only to wear your favorite go-to comfy clothes during the majority of your trip? Packing for college is kind of like that, except your student will have these extra items to deal with in their dorm room for months. There's no need to take the entire wardrobe. But keep the climate of the college location in mind. Make plans to switch seasonal clothing during fall break and spring break, if appropriate.

There's also no need to fill the limited space with enough snacks, toiletries, or laundry supplies for the entire semester. Bring enough supplies on move-in day to get your student through the first few weeks. This will give them time to determine what they use on a regular basis.

Care packages are a great way to not only send necessities to your student, but also let them know you are thinking about them. Whether a large box or an envelope with a restaurant or coffee gift card, students love to receive mail from home. Care packages are a nice way to celebrate the completion of a project, send good luck wishes as your student prepares for exams, or surprise them with a "just because." You might toss in something for your student's room-mate too. Share your student's address with family members who would like to send an encouraging word, and maybe $20 as well.

Talk about ways your student will restock on necessities. Will they have a car on campus, or does the institution provide a shuttle service? Are there stores within walking distance of your student's dorm? You may be able to take advantage of a local grocery or box store that provides online ordering. Place the order and throw in a few healthy/ fresh items, pay online, and your student simply has to pick it up. This also works well for students who haven't quite gotten the hang of budgeting just yet.

### Information to Watch For

When reading the information provided by your student's university, look for:

## What to bring

And often more importantly, what *not* to bring. Twin XL sheets are a thing; be sure to confirm the bed size in your student's residence hall. Heaters, small appliances with heating elements, and extension cords are often on the list of what not to bring. Be sure to check out restrictions before spending money on these things.

## Specifics about the room

Pay special attention to the layout and dimensions. When shopping for storage items, keep in mind the amount of floor, hanging, drawer, under-bed, and wall space available in the room. Save receipts and don't remove price tags until you see if the items will be used. Open and test new items before taking them to campus. This could save frustration on move-in day. No one wants to discover a dent or missing pieces while unpacking a new refrigerator. Additional questions to consider include:

- Is there a sink in your student's room? This will determine storage needs for toiletries.

- What is provided (e.g., desk, chair, lamp, trash can, window coverings)? Think about seating options other than the bed. A folding/camping chair may come in handy for guests and outdoor events.

- Does the university-supplied furniture have to stay in the room? Furniture will likely be assessed upon move-out, so make a plan before swapping out the supplied chair.

## Housing FAQs

Look for answers to the following questions:

- How can my student connect with their roommate before move-in?

- What areas are students expected to clean? What cleaning supplies are provided?

- Can you ship large items to campus instead of traveling with them on move-in day?

- What stores are close to campus for last-minute shopping?

- Is there a common room or kitchen? What items (e.g., coffee maker, refrigerator, microwave, utensils and plates) are available there?

- Where is the laundry room, how many machines are there, and how much does it cost to wash and dry a load? Do the machines take quarters, tokens, cards?

- Are there printers available in the residence hall or the library?

## Helping Your Student Pack

You can certainly help them pack, but make sure they are doing the heavy lifting. Your student should be responsible for making choices about what to bring, but may need you to remind them to pack the socks without holes and to include school supplies, not just video games. Helping them pack is a good time to initiate important conversations. If their hands are busy and you aren't making eye contact, you may find your student will open up to you. Revisit a topic you've been wanting to bring up or take a deep breath and address something specific to your family. Another ideal time to initiate a conversation is when you and your student are out shopping. Have your student drive so they won't be snuggled in the passenger seat staring at their phone. Trust your gut in that moment and lean into whatever comes to your heart and mind.

## The Basic Packing List

Many of the specifics will depend on the university and your student's preferences and needs, but here are some ideas to get you started:

### Room set-up and decor

- [ ] Storage containers (under-bed drawers/containers can be a great idea)
- [ ] Desk lamp
- [ ] Fan (could go home at Thanksgiving to save space)
- [ ] Alarm clock (if a phone alarm isn't enough to wake up your student)
- [ ] Dry erase board for door
- [ ] Door stop (a door propped open is a great way to meet hallmates!)
- [ ] Command strips/hooks
- [ ] Photos and posters
- [ ] Small tool kit

### Linens and laundry supplies

- [ ] Two sets of sheets (college beds typically require twin XL sheets)
- [ ] Comforter
- [ ] Pillow(s)
- [ ] Mattress pad (check college regulations)
- [ ] Two sets of towels and washcloths
- [ ] Clothes hangers

- ☐ Laundry bag/basket (consider the space in the room in deciding how laundry should be stored and carried)
- ☐ Detergent/dryer sheets/stain remover
- ☐ Fold-up clothes drying rack

## Clothing (remind your student to pack only what they will actually wear)

- ☐ Enough socks and underwear to last two weeks (between trips to the laundry room)
- ☐ Jeans/pants
- ☐ Shirts, sweaters, t-shirts
- ☐ Sweats, comfy clothes, and pajamas
- ☐ Athletic wear/swimsuit
- ☐ Slippers
- ☐ Two jackets (light and heavy)
- ☐ Raincoat/umbrella
- ☐ Winter gear (hats, mittens, scarves, boots), as appropriate
- ☐ Sneakers/comfortable shoes
- ☐ Sandals
- ☐ 1 or 2 business casual outfits (for interviews, presentations, and dates)
- ☐ Jewelry (leave the valuables at home)
- ☐ Sunglasses

## Toiletries and necessities

- ☐ Shower caddy
- ☐ Shower shoes

- ☐ Bathrobe
- ☐ Tissues
- ☐ Personal hygiene items (e.g., shampoo, toothpaste, feminine products, tweezers)
- ☐ First aid kit (e.g., prescriptions, pain reliever, Band-Aids, cold medicine)

## Household and kitchen supplies

- ☐ Microwave safe bowl, plate, cup, silverware (no more than two each)
- ☐ To-go coffee mug
- ☐ Water bottle
- ☐ Food storage containers
- ☐ Non-perishable snacks
- ☐ Paper towels
- ☐ Trash bags
- ☐ All-purpose cleaner
- ☐ Dish soap
- ☐ Sponge/rag
- ☐ Wet wipes
- ☐ Hand sanitizer
- ☐ Disinfectant spray/odor eliminator
- ☐ Flashlight

## Electronics

- ☐ Computer

- ☐ Speakers
- ☐ Headphones
- ☐ Chargers for all devices
- ☐ Power strips
- ☐ TV (streaming on a computer will save space)

## School supplies

- ☐ Backpack
- ☐ Highlighters (multiple colors)
- ☐ Pens/pencils
- ☐ Notebooks
- ☐ Post-it notes
- ☐ Scissors
- ☐ Tape
- ☐ Stapler

## Identification

- ☐ Driver's license or state-issued ID
- ☐ Forms needed for employment (e.g., passport, birth certificate, social security card)
- ☐ Student ID
- ☐ Insurance cards
- ☐ Debit/credit cards

## Things to Leave at Home

While this list will vary by college, here are some common items that are not allowed or won't be needed:

- Kitchen appliances
- Electric blankets
- Space heaters
- Extension cords
- Iron and ironing board (strong guarantee it won't be used)
- Halogen lamps
- Tapestries or fabric wall hangings
- Candles, incense, or anything that creates an open flame
- Pets
- Valuable jewelry or other sentimental items
- More than two high school t-shirts (trust us; they'll get many college t-shirts soon)
- Too much of anything (think minimally!)

## See the Empty Room as a Blank Canvas

Even though you're spending all summer (and longer) preparing for the moment, stepping into your student's new home for the next year may be a shock. Prepare yourself before you enter the room for the first time. You may see block walls, cold floors, and few electrical outlets and have to fight the urge to drop the storage totes full of neatly folded towels, grab your grown "baby," and run for the nearest exit. Your student, on the other hand, may be filled with a sense of excitement for what's to come. So bite your tongue and use your nervous energy to dig in and start cleaning and organizing. By the time your student has unpacked a few totes and hung some posters, you'll be surprised how much better you feel about their new home.

## Closing Advice

Packing for college should be a fun experience. This is an opportunity for your student to show off their adulting skills and take the lead in making the lists, choosing the bedding, and packing themselves. Help make sure they are referring to the university's packing list and connecting with their roommate about any large items. While they might think they need every last t-shirt, remind them that less is more and they can always swap out clothes at Thanksgiving.

---

### Conversation Starters

- What items are on your school's packing list?
- What will you need to make your room a comfortable space?
- What is your decorating style?
- Have you connected with your roommate about who will bring larger items?
- Have you talked to your roommate about your living style and how you will balance your individual needs?

---

## Chapter 11

# WHAT IF I CRY WHILE SAYING GOODBYE?

How to move your student in and say goodbye

**Nicki Jenkins**
**University of Kentucky**

Move-in day has finally arrived! You've spent months helping your student prepare for this significant life transition. You've made sure they've packed everything they might need to be successful at the college of their choice. You've had important conversations about financial and academic expectations and how to ask for help when needed. You feel confident in the young adult you have raised and are excited to see them take this next step.

The anticipation has been building and now, on move-in day, you finally get to see all that hard work come to fruition and celebrate all you've accomplished together. Shedding a few tears of joy is to be expected. So how can you ensure that your student's move-in experience runs smoothly and is satisfying for all involved, while still managing emotions? The answer, like most things in college, is to do your homework, show up on time, and be flexible.

## Read Your Move-in Instructions

Just like you, your student's college has been planning move-in day for months. It's considered the best traffic patterns, parking options, and check-in procedures, and it's most likely recruited half of campus to assist with unloading vehicles. It has probably outlined in detail what you can expect when you arrive and how best to navigate the process through a list of instructions.

Every university has a different process for moving students to campus. Some things you will want to watch for include:

- Are students given a time slot or do they get to choose a slot?
- Is there an allotted amount of time to unload?
- Are there limits on how many guests/cars each student can bring?
- Which directions do you have to follow based on the hall your student is moving into?
- Will you park your car and move in or is it a drop-and-drive system?

To avoid unnecessary stress, pay close attention to all communications regarding move-in day and be sure to familiarize yourself with the tips, procedures, and suggestions outlined in the instructions.

Students living in off-campus housing will need to refer to their contract or lease agreement to verify policies and procedures surrounding move-in. Be sure to encourage your student to read their housing documentation closely to ensure their move-in dates and times align with any required campus orientation events, scheduled college traditions, and first classes.

## Let Your Student Take the Lead

Move-in day is a great time to encourage your student to take responsibility for making decisions while you are still physically there to support them as needed. Before you even leave home, ask your student who they would like to bring along for move-in (e.g., siblings, friends, additional family), how they would like your help, and how long they would like you to stick around after they have settled in. Having these conversations early can help ease some of the tension that may arise as you navigate the day.

Once you arrive, allow your student to take the lead by introducing themselves to university staff and other students and checking themselves into their assigned residence hall. Don't be afraid to ask your student questions throughout the day, but allow them to be the liaison between you and university staff so that they may begin to develop a rapport. In addition to asking good questions, be sure to listen and process carefully the information that is given so as to not miss important details. You may want to bring a small notepad or open a new note on your phone to jot down information throughout the day.

When it comes to unpacking, let your student take the lead and communicate their needs to you as they arise. Allow your student to unpack their room and organize it in a way that makes sense to them, even if it may take a little longer than you think it should. Your student will let you know when they need your help and will probably even be happy to delegate some of the unpacking burden to someone else. Most students will be thrilled to let you make the bed. Remember, your student may have been dreaming of what their college room will look like for a while and the process of making that dream a reality will help them feel more at home in their new surroundings.

## Pack Your Patience

Students respond to move-in day in a variety of ways and their reactions may surprise you. Some students have no problem being flexible as they navigate the organized chaos of the day while maintaining a positive attitude. For others who crave predictability and order, the hustle and bustle of moving in with hundreds of their peers may feel overwhelming. The feeling of being overwhelmed might result in their speaking more sharply than you would like or more emotionally than even they were expecting.

Your student is trying to manage a host of emotions while keeping their composure and processing this huge life change; they simply may not be thinking about how they need to communicate with family. It's extremely important to have conversations beforehand about how to best communicate with one another throughout the day in order to prepare for whatever response your student may have and protect yourselves from unnecessary arguments. And remember, the best way to show your support is to maintain a positive attitude and to demonstrate patience. When you are packing your vehicle with all your student's belongings, be sure to pack a little extra patience for your student, yourself, and the staff supporting the process. Remember as you are moving in one student, staff are moving in thousands.

## Celebrate the Occasion

Sometimes it can seem like preparations for your student's move to college have overwhelmed all aspects of your family's life and home: there are mounds of paperwork, boxes of belongings, and piles of laundry, to say nothing of the scheduled orientations and meetings during family time and extra personal attention for your college student. When it's finally time for your student to move to college, take a breath and celebrate how significant and impactful this experience will be for both your student and your family. Involve other siblings or family members in creating moments of celebration and encouragement before your student leaves, whether that is through a family send-off celebration, a special dinner at home, or a family tradition.

Continue to look for opportunities to celebrate and make memories throughout the move-in process. Create a meaningful road trip playlist to listen to on your way to campus. Take your student out to eat at a local restaurant near the campus before you head home. Take a family picture on campus or attend a college-sponsored event together. Taking advantage of those special moments can help students and families feel a sense of closure while still looking forward to what's ahead.

## Cry If You Need To

While dropping your student off at college, you may experience a rush of emotions. After all, you have been with your student every step of the way for the last 17+ years and have now sent them off to tackle the world. It's perfectly reasonable to assume that you may experience feelings of pride, excitement, and hope while also feelings of loss, sorrow, and fear. If those conflicting feelings produce a few tears, so be it! There is no shame in crying throughout the process or at the end of an intense and meaningful day.

Just be conscious of how your emotions may influence your student's feelings about leaving home and their family and starting a new life in college. Try to mirror your student's emotions throughout the day and when you say goodbye. If your student cries, then cry with them. If your student is not one to show emotions, try to hold back your tears until the car ride home. Leave campus on a positive note so your student can focus their attention on connecting to their new campus community rather than missing what they've left behind.

The car ride home is a great time to reminisce, talk about how proud you are of your student, and even open the tear floodgates, if need be. You may want to consider scheduling a fun activity directly after dropping your student off at college as a way to continue the celebration. Focusing on enjoying your trip home may help alleviate some of the temporary heartache you may experience. This is also a good time to turn your attention on any siblings who came along.

Once you return home, it may be tempting to check in with your student immediately. However, it is important to give your student space during the first few days and weeks of college. Sometimes it takes a little while for students to get their bearings and feel like they belong; checking in too often might give them an avenue for expressing negative feelings about their college experience before they have given it a real chance. Talk with your student beforehand about expectations around communication during those first few weeks and let them take the lead. Read more tips about how to support your student from home in chapter 12.

## Closing Advice

No matter which university your student selects, moving in should be a time of celebration for the whole family. Enjoy each moment and take every opportunity to create memories and include loved ones in the process, especially younger siblings. Your student will remember their first day on campus forever and will cherish the opportunity to experience that day with their family, even if it doesn't always seem like they cherish you in the moment. Remember to prepare by reading through all move-in instructions and having conversations around communication and expectations during the move-in process. Let your student take the lead and exercise extra patience as they navigate their new campus home. And once the day is done, take a deep breath and remember to congratulate yourself and your student on all the hard work that went into making sure they are exactly where they need to be. Well done!

## Conversation Starters

- Has your school sent specific move-in instructions?

- How would you like me to help on move-in day? What tasks can I take care of for you?

- What is your orientation/welcome week schedule like on move-in day?

- What are some signs that we should take a break while moving you in?

- How can we celebrate the big move before we hit the road?

- How much is "too much" communication between us during your first week on campus?

# Chapter 12
# WHAT IF MY STUDENT DOESN'T NEED ME NOW?

## How to show support during the first semester

**Brie Jutte Waterman**
**University of Colorado Boulder**

Your student is officially at college now and the question starts to sink in…"What if my student doesn't need me now?" We are here to tell you, they do! College students still need their parents, families, and support systems. This chapter will dive into how you can stay engaged and support your student navigating this transition.

## The Ups and the Downs

The entire summer leading up to the first semester has been a transition, and it likely had its ups and downs. The transition doesn't end when you drop your student off in their dorm or on the first day of classes. Once they have officially become a college student, they might feel a rollercoaster of emotions. They start off with the excitement of orientation and meeting new people, but after the first few weeks when the "honeymoon phase" wears off, it is easy for them to feel overwhelmed. Normalize their emotions and help them understand that it's okay to have conflicting feelings. They may experience feelings of homesickness, even if they love their college experience. They will miss the comfort of their old life and friends, even when they are having fun exploring new activities.

You may want to talk with your student about not comparing their college journey to others. Pointing out that social media is always a display of the "highlight reels" is a good conversation to have. Their friends will be posting pictures with new friends and new experiences in their college towns, which may make your student feel like they are missing out or not doing enough. Remind them that no one is posting the behind the scenes moments, such as misunderstanding the instructions on the washing machine or not getting the grade they were expecting.

## Making Friends

If your student lives on campus, encourage them to stay on campus until the first break (often Thanksgiving). It can be tempting to travel home for those first couple of weekends. However, the first couple of months are the best time to meet new people. Over the weekend is when students will socialize and when college really starts to feel like home for new students.

During the first few weeks of a school year, many student clubs and organizations have an involvement fair or showcase. Encourage your student to put themselves out there and try out a new club or two. They might feel uncomfortable or vulnerable showing up to a club meeting, but reassure your student that this is how every student starts off their college journey and it will be worth it!

Making friends takes time. The people your student first meets at orientation or a hall meeting might become lifelong friends, or they may be merely the group that helps them acclimate to college. Sometimes students don't solidify a core group of friends until they get deeper into their major or find the club that best fits their area of interest. Remind your student of how diverse their past friendships were and encourage them to be open to new experiences.

## The Family Role

You and your student are in this together. You are partners in this process, even as your student matures and becomes the driver of their experience. They are steering the vehicle and making the ultimate decisions, but you provide navigation and support.

One major theme in this book is open communication, and creating a communications plan with your student. While it is helpful to make a plan before your student heads off to school, remember that you will have to be flexible and expect adjustments as they better understand their college life and schedule. Once they get settled into their new routine, it might be easy for them to get caught up in their new life and forget to check in. Unanswered texts and missed calls piling up can leave you feeling uneasy. Decide before they leave for college how often you would like to hear from them, and discuss your expectations around check-ins and deeper conversations. Maybe it is a Snapchat a day, a text message at night, or a FaceTime call on the weekends. Remember that there is no right way to communicate, and your plan will change over time.

As you communicate with your student throughout the semester, think about all of the topics covered in previous chapters and when would be good times for reminders. Big weekend events—such as homecoming—are a good time for reminders about personal safety, drinking, and drug use. October is a great time to ask your student if their budget is still on track and to make adjustments if necessary. If they haven't found a campus job in the first month, ask about what positions they have applied for. Offer to review their application or resume, or suggest they visit the employment office or career center. Midterms is the perfect time to check in about study habits and time management, where they are struggling, and to remind them to use their professors' office hours.

While talking with your student, it is important to ask open-ended questions and keep in mind persistence. Sometimes you might only be one "no" or "yes" away from them opening up and telling you more.

Also remember that, as a parent, you often hear the worst things, as your student relies on you for a listening ear. Let them vent and use leading questions to learn more. Your student might be relying on you to support them through those tough times, but remember that they are also likely experiencing good times they aren't sharing with you.

## Finding and Using Resources

Sometimes your student might need you to encourage them to advocate for themselves. Self-advocacy is the ability to tell people what you want and need in a thoughtful, straightforward, and clear way. Advocating for themselves is the most direct way for students to secure the changes they need. Not only are parents often not able to make calls and decisions for their college students, but self-advocacy is also an important life skill that everyone needs to learn. You can support this by helping your student understand the root of the issue on their mind, resources that might be available, and questions to ask when they reach out to staff.

There are many people on campus who care about your student's well-being. It can be hard for you, as a family member, to feel you are aware of all the available resources. You don't need to remember every nuance. The important thing is to read any information that comes your way and be prepared to assist your student as needed. As you've already been reading about, some of the primary support resources for students include:

- **Academics.** Your student's academic advisor helps them stay on track. Their professors and TAs are another resource. Your student might feel unsure about using office hours at first, but encourage them to take advantage of this time. If your student has a concern about their coursework or grade, or even a personal issue that is impacting their academic performance, they should feel comfortable letting their advisor and/or professor know. Remind your student to refer to the course syllabus when working with a professor! (See chapter 4 for more academic support resources.)

- **Finances.** Financial offices provide aid and scholarships and collect payments, but staff are also there to answer questions and help you understand the process and find additional support as needed. (See chapter 5 for more financial resources.)

- **Residence Life.** Resident advisors (RAs) are experienced students who live in halls to support student residents. They will likely organize educational and social programming for their halls, but are also there as a support if students have questions. Professional Residence Life staff can also help students and parents with housing and residential living concerns.

- **Wellness.** If your student is feeling stressed or sick, learn about the college's health and counseling services available on campus. Help them understand the value of choosing healthy dining options and taking advantage of the gym. (See chapter 6 for more health and wellness resources.)

No matter who on campus students are reaching out to for help, it is a good idea that they go into the meetings with a plan, possible solutions, and questions. If your student is struggling to self-advocate or not getting the support they need, they can see if their college has an ombuds office, office of case management, or another office that helps students find resources to solve particular problems.

All of these resources, staff, and faculty are there to help you, your student, and your family feel connected and supported during this journey. If at any time you don't know where to go for information, check to see if the institution has a parent & family programs office. Staff in these offices can usually answer your questions and help you get connected to other key areas.

## Closing Advice

Bottom line...your student still needs you! You are there to help guide them. They will experience ups and downs, and you're likely to hear mostly about the downs. Your questions and words of advice will help them adjust and find community at school.

---

### Conversation Starters

- What is your homework like compared to high school homework?
- What are your professors like compared to your high school teachers?
- Have you joined any student groups?
- How are you making new friends?
- What is happening on campus this weekend?

---

# Chapter 13

# HOW MUCH LAUNDRY
# DID YOU BRING?

How to plan for the first visit home

**Libby Daggers**
**Texas A&M University**

The first six weeks of a student's transition to the collegiate environment are crucial. Students begin to acclimate to their new surroundings during these first few weeks and start building connections on campus. While students may express interest in visiting home during their first few weeks, it is vital to encourage them (especially if they're homesick) to spend these weeks on campus working toward establishing themselves. Around the time both you and your student get used to the separation, it will be time for them to visit home. Depending on your proximity to your student's college or university, their first visit home might be for a weekend or an extended break.

There is a lot of excitement and anticipation for you, your student, and any siblings at home before the first visit. Many families envision a blissful weekend full of one-on-one bonding time with their student. While that dream may come true, it is important to temper expectations. This first time home can disappoint and frustrate you if there is no clear communication ahead of time. Discussing expectations can ensure a more positive experience for everyone, since the most obvious challenge families face is unmanaged expectations.

For that reason, a few weeks before your student comes home, you should be sure to check in about their visit. In this chapter you will find several suggestions, inspired by parents who have been in your shoes, to help the first visit go smoothly.

## Acknowledge the Need to Recharge

"Students often view home as a refuge from the madness of college life. Let your home be that refuge. Give them their space to relax and decompress. Have their favorite foods and other familiar treats available. Expect that they may want to do little, except visit with their friends." —Parent of a college student

Discuss your respective plans for the visit. If there are certain family events you have planned and expect your student to attend, make sure you tell them up front. At the same time, understand that your student will want to make plans of their own with friends, so ask them what they have in mind. While creating an overly structured schedule is probably not the best solution, an open conversation about plans allows everyone to be on the same page.

It is also important not to over-schedule your student's visit. While you may imagine a time filled with family meals and activities, do not be surprised if your student spends a lot of time in their room by themselves and sleeps more than they used to. Students experience a significant transition during their first semester as they make adjustments to many areas of their lives. These changes often mean more academic stress and time spent on schoolwork, involvement in new extracurricular activities, and a new schedule that often means staying up late and sleeping in late. The first visit home for many students is a much-needed respite from their new environment, when they can look forward to catching up on rest and recharging themselves. For some, going to college is the first time they share a room with someone, which means coming home to their own rooms offers the first extended time to be alone.

## Talk about Household Rules and Responsibilities

"Start with the rules in place when your student left." —Parent of a college student

"Give them more freedom than they had in high school, but also set some 'adult' rules, such as deadlines to be home by, use of family car(s), etc." —Parent of a college student

In addition to discussing plans, you should also revisit any house rules or expectations you had for your student during high school. For example, will you expect them to follow the same curfew you had set for them in high school? Remember, your student has spent the past several weeks or months being able to come and go as they please. It is often a hard adjustment for students to come home and be told they must be in the house by 10 p.m. While you don't have to let them stay out all night, is there a compromise you can make to show you recognize their newfound independence?

If your student doesn't have their own car, you will need to talk about access to a vehicle while they are home. Do they need to ask you before taking the vehicle? Do you need them to schedule when they need it and let you know where they are going?

What chores will they have to do while at home? Do you expect them to contribute in any specific ways? In these scenarios, it helps to find the delicate balance between "my house, my rules" and honoring the independence of your college student. They may be expecting a leisurely break where they are not responsible for any housework. If you want them to do the dishes, you should let them know.

## Prepare for Changes

"Be aware that this is not the 'child' you dropped off in August. They have had a few months of independent living. Not to say that they shouldn't live by the house rules when they return, but you just need to realize that you're dealing with more of an adult now." —Parent of a college student

A lot can happen in the first few weeks away from home. Your student may have new and different interests. They may be following a new diet and no longer eat a favorite family dish. They may come home with a new piercing, tattoo, or hair color. Any of these things may catch you off guard unless you include these topics as part of your conversation before the visit. Ask your student to be open with you about any changes so that you are not surprised.

At the same time, you will likely be astonished at how much your student has grown since they left. While your student is home, look for meaningful ways for them to show their independence. If they have a new interest in cooking, ask them to help you prepare a meal for the family. Your student may have started a new exercise routine or joined a new sport in their free time. Take the time to learn about their new daily routine and join in if you can while they are visiting.

## Enjoy Your Conversations

"As parents, do your best to appreciate all of the 'new' experiences your student tells you about. An interested audience leads to much more sharing. Helping them navigate through their thoughts on the positives and negatives in their new world will help them feel refreshed and ready to hit the ground running when they go back to school." —Parent of a college student

Your student's visit home is an excellent opportunity to learn more about their experiences at college. Although you may feel very knowledgeable about what's been going on so far, they may open up more to you when you are sitting together in person compared to when you talk on the phone or text. As your student shares information about their life at school, listen intently. Try to ask open-ended questions. Your curiosity about what they are learning in classes will get you far more information than asking about their grades.

Ask about how they are engaging in the campus community. Ask about student organizations, jobs, and other opportunities outside of the classroom. Your student is likely to share both positive and negative aspects of their experience so far. Do not take these moments for granted. Supporting your student as they navigate feelings about college so far is essential for their success.

## Closing Advice

There is a chance that, even after reading this chapter, your visit does not go perfectly. If you run into a problem, don't let that one conflict ruin the entire visit. Try your best to recover and make the most of your time together. It is also important to remember this time together should be enjoyable for everyone involved. Your tendency may be to take care of your student the entire time they are home. You may want to cook all their meals, do all their laundry, clean up after them, etc. Hypothetically, your student has been doing this for themselves while on campus. So, when you ask them how much laundry they brought home...it's okay to make them do it themselves. You don't want to look back on your time together and realize you spent most of it in the laundry room.

## Conversation Starters

- What plans have you made with friends for when you're home?

- How would you like to spend time with the family?

- What homework will you have to do while you're home?

- What snacks would you like me to have on hand for you?

- Have you made any big changes in your diet or appearance we should know about?

# Conclusion

In 2020, many college administrators learned something that those in parent and family programs have known for years: parents and family are critical members of the campus community. You helped your student persevere through a pandemic, you led them through the college search and admission process, you are ready to walk them through summer preparation, and you will continue to give them love and support throughout their educational journey.

Remember, you are not alone. Every staff and faculty member at the university is there for one reason: your student. They care about them, want them to succeed, and are here to help them get to their next big milestone: their college commencement ceremony.

They also care about you, the parents and family members who are cheering your student on from home. As you've read throughout this book, staff members are happy to talk with parents and help you navigate the process. When you call, remember these tips:

- Start with kindness. Staff members truly want to help, and will do their best to get you the information you need.

- Try to assume the best. Chances are, the situation isn't as dire as the picture your student paints. Students vent to parents, but the food really isn't all that bad and one bad grade will not ruin their life. Keep an open mind as you help your student determine if the situation is a true emergency.

- Keep your trust. In your student, in staff, and in yourself.

When calling their student's university, parents frequently start with, "I don't want to be a helicopter parent, but..." You've seen the harmful spin that the media has put on college parenting, and you don't want to fall into that negative stereotype. But here's the secret: helicopters are very useful tools. They have a big view and can see things that those on the ground can't see. They can get to an emergency quickly and bring help. But once help has arrived, they go back up. Don't be afraid to be this kind of helicopter.

You've survived the college search and decision process. You've conquered the checklists. You've squirmed through the tough conversations. Your student is packed and ready to launch. Congratulations, parents! You are definitely College Ready!

# Appendix 1
## CHECKLISTS

Use these checklists throughout the summer to help you get everything done. Be sure to check communications from your student's college for university-specific lists.

## Calendars and Communication

- [ ] Choose a weekly college planning check-in time
- [ ] Create a shared calendar with important dates (e.g., orientation, room selection, move-in)
- [ ] Mark family time on shared calendar
- [ ] List all forms/tasks that are required over the summer and their due dates
- [ ] Encourage your student to familiarize themselves with various campus support offices
- [ ] Encourage family bonding time, particularly with younger siblings

---

## Technology and Access

- [ ] Make sure your student regularly checks their university email for important information, key dates, and action items

- [ ] Discuss with your student which aspects of their educational records you expect access to (e.g., finances, grades)

- [ ] Discover what "proxy" access process is in place and how to transfer permission

- [ ] Discover if a parent portal is available at your student's institution

- [ ] Remind your student to keep passwords private, even from you

---

## Academics

- [ ] Sign up for and complete new student and family orientation

- [ ] Encourage your student to connect with their academic advisor about course registration

- [ ] Research how to purchase textbooks

- [ ] Help your student apply for any needed assistance (e.g., disability-related accommodations)

- [ ] Ask your student what department their major is in, as well as what college their department is in

- [ ] Learn about academic support services on campus

---

## Finances

- ☐ Submit the FAFSA
- ☐ Look through the breakdown of costs; understand what fees cover and how often they will be charged
- ☐ Research additional scholarship opportunities to help cover costs
- ☐ Have your student accept any awards offered by the university
- ☐ Help your student understand the value of their education, how much out-of-pocket expenses are each year, and what loan repayment will look like upon graduation
- ☐ Establish expectations around whether you will provide money, how often, and what responsibilities are associated with it
- ☐ Help your student begin to research campus jobs
- ☐ Set up a local bank account for your student if needed
- ☐ Make sure you are able to access student financial accounts information if you are paying the bill
- ☐ Pay the first semester bill

---

## Health, Wellness, and Safety

- ☐ Ask your student to fill out emergency contact information in their student account
- ☐ Complete any annual clinician appointments over the summer

- [ ] Make sure your student completes and submits the required immunizations
- [ ] Submit documentation if needing accommodations on campus
- [ ] Check to see if your health insurance is accepted on campus
- [ ] Obtain a supply of maintenance medications for three months or get a prescription to be filled at a pharmacy convenient to campus
- [ ] Help your student make a list of prescriptions on their phone
- [ ] Create a small first aid kit that includes frequently used medications (with directions) and a thermometer
- [ ] Help your student research safety apps and phone numbers at their college
- [ ] Locate websites for the departments that can help if something goes wrong, including student health center, student counseling center, safety department, and Title IX office
- [ ] Find and review the college's policies on alcohol and drug use
- [ ] Familiarize yourself with state and local laws about alcohol and drugs
- [ ] Find and review reporting resources for students to report sexual violence
- [ ] Find how you can report that you are concerned about your student

---

## Adulting and Relationship Building

- ☐ Encourage your student to practice adult responsibilities (e.g., making doctor appointments)
- ☐ Make sure your student understands basic skills in laundry, cooking, cleaning, car maintenance, and budgeting
- ☐ Talk to your student about the diversity they will encounter at college, differences along the lines of race, culture, religion, gender expression, sexuality, personal values, and ability
- ☐ Make sure your student connects with their roommate prior to move-in
- ☐ Encourage your student to explore campus engagement opportunities

## Packing, Move-in, and Commuting

- ☐ Make plans for goodbyes early
- ☐ Find the university's packing list and use it as a guide while shopping
- ☐ Book your hotel early, as hotels near campus will often fill up around move-in day
- ☐ Bring only the essentials and prepare to swap out on breaks as necessary
- ☐ Read move-in instructions carefully so that you understand what to expect
- ☐ Print any necessary materials, such as parking passes or luggage tags

- ☐ Map your route to campus
- ☐ Know where to go once you arrive on campus—look for specific routes in move-in instructions
- ☐ Pack any necessary move-in day tools or equipment such as your own dolly and basic tools (e.g., measuring tape, screwdriver)
- ☐ Pack water and snacks
- ☐ Make a "to-do" list (both needed tasks and fun) for your time on campus
- ☐ Help your commuter student understand the best way to get to campus and what to do if a back-up is needed
- ☐ Encourage your commuter student to make a community on campus and spend time there outside of class

---

## Ongoing Support

- ☐ Look for parent and family programs office or other family-specific resources
- ☐ Sign up for parent newsletters (if available)
- ☐ Make a communication plan with your student and discuss how often you will call, text, or video chat during the first few weeks
- ☐ Learn about your student's experience through open-ended questions
- ☐ Normalize experiencing homesickness and ups and downs of the transition
- ☐ Encourage your student to self-advocate when issues arise

- [ ] Look for campus events for families such as family weekend or family day
- [ ] Check with your student about their calendar before planning a visit to campus
- [ ] Show your support and school pride
- [ ] Send your student a card or care package

---

## Visits Home

- [ ] Have your student's room ready
- [ ] Stock your student's favorite foods and snacks
- [ ] Plan some of your student's favorite hometown activities
- [ ] Ask if your student will have homework to complete while home
- [ ] Discuss the plan for their time at home in advance, including expectations about family time, household responsibilities and rules, and curfews
- [ ] Make your student aware of any changes at home prior to their arrival
- [ ] Ask if your student has made any big changes in their diet or appearance that you should be aware of

---

## Appendix 2
# PACKING LIST

Be sure to check the university's packing list to guide you as you shop and pack. This list is a starting point; fill in items specific to your student.

## Room Set-Up and Decor

☐ Storage containers

☐ Desk lamp

☐ Fan

☐ Alarm clock

☐ Dry erase board for door

☐ Door stop

☐ Command strips/hooks

☐ Photos and posters

☐ Small tool kit

_____

## Linens and Laundry Supplies

- ☐ Two sets of sheets (college beds typically require twin XL sheets)
- ☐ Comforter
- ☐ Pillow(s)
- ☐ Mattress pad (check college regulations)
- ☐ Two sets of towels and washcloths
- ☐ Clothes hangers
- ☐ Laundry bag/basket
- ☐ Detergent/dryer sheets/stain remover
- ☐ Fold-up clothes drying rack

---

## Clothing

- ☐ Socks
- ☐ Underwear
- ☐ Jeans/pants
- ☐ Shirts, sweaters, t-shirts
- ☐ Sweats/comfy clothes
- ☐ Pajamas
- ☐ Athletic wear
- ☐ Swimsuit
- ☐ Slippers
- ☐ Two jackets (light and heavy)
- ☐ Raincoat

- ☐ Umbrella
- ☐ Winter hat
- ☐ Mittens
- ☐ Scarf
- ☐ Boots
- ☐ Sneakers
- ☐ Comfortable shoes
- ☐ Sandals
- ☐ 1 or 2 business casual outfits
- ☐ Jewelry (leave the valuables at home)
- ☐ Sunglasses

---

## Toiletries and Necessities

- ☐ Shower caddy
- ☐ Shower shoes
- ☐ Bathrobe
- ☐ Tissues
- ☐ Personal hygiene items
- ☐ Shampoo
- ☐ Conditioner
- ☐ Soap
- ☐ Facewash
- ☐ Toothpaste
- ☐ Toothbrush

- [ ] Floss
- [ ] Deodorant
- [ ] Comb/brush
- [ ] Tweezers
- [ ] Nail clippers
- [ ] Hair styling products
- [ ] Hair dryer
- [ ] Hair straightener/curling iron
- [ ] Cosmetics
- [ ] Feminine products
- [ ] Razor and shaving cream
- [ ] Lotion
- [ ] Sunscreen
- [ ] Cotton swabs
- [ ] First aid kit
- [ ] Prescriptions
- [ ] Pain reliever
- [ ] Band-Aids
- [ ] Cold medicine
- [ ] Cough drops
- [ ] Vitamins
- [ ] Antacid
- [ ] Allergy relief
- [ ] Eye drops

_____

## Household and Kitchen Supplies

- ☐ Microwave safe bowl, plate, cup, silverware (no more than two each)
- ☐ To-go coffee mug
- ☐ Water bottle
- ☐ Food storage containers
- ☐ Non-perishable snacks
- ☐ Paper towels
- ☐ Trash bags
- ☐ All-purpose cleaner
- ☐ Dish soap
- ☐ Sponge/rag
- ☐ Wet wipes
- ☐ Hand sanitizer
- ☐ Disinfectant spray/odor eliminator
- ☐ Flashlight

---

## Electronics

- ☐ Computer
- ☐ Speakers
- ☐ Headphones
- ☐ Chargers for all devices
- ☐ Power strips
- ☐ TV

## School Supplies

- ☐ Backpack
- ☐ Highlighters (multiple colors)
- ☐ Pens/pencils
- ☐ Notebooks
- ☐ Post-it notes
- ☐ Scissors
- ☐ Tape
- ☐ Stapler

## Identification

- ☐ Driver's license or state-issued ID
- ☐ Forms needed for employment
- ☐ Student ID
- ☐ Insurance cards
- ☐ Debit/credit cards

CPSIA information can be obtained
at www.ICGtesting.com
Printed in the USA
FSHW011819100621

9 781736 918234